MW01169480

Legendary East St. Louisans

An African American Series

Legendary East St. Louisans
An African American Series

Reginald Petty and Tiffany Lee

TIFFANYROSE Publishing

Second Edition

Front Cover: Picture of Bruce and Helen Petty
Front Cover Design: Tiffany Lee
Picture on Page ii: Professor B.F. Bowles and teachers
Publisher Contact:editor@tiffanyrosepublishing.com
https://www.facebook.com/TiffanyRosePublishing
ICUROSE

Copyright © 2016
All rights reserved.
ISBN-13: 978-1533512772
ISBN-10: 1533512779

PREFACE

Who am I! Who are we! For African-Americans on this continent our past is as unique as are our experiences. Since our arrival on American soil, constant attempts have been made by Europeans to extinguish our past, our contributions, and our rich cultural history.

The purpose of this book is to bring forth the history of African American East St. Louisans, and their uniqueness as well as their positive contributions to humanity. In 1886, East St. Louis was developed as a town in Illinois, right across the river from St. Louis, Missouri. Although the population never exceeded much more than 100,000, it was a major center for cattle, stockyards, railroads and many businesses such as Aluminum Ore, The Glass House, etc.

African-Americans were present in East St. Louis before and during its creation, however most were considered unequal and sub-human. History has proven Whites wrong of their assumption. There is no part of the United States History that can be explained without the inclusion of African-Americans. East St. Louis has definitely produced its share of productive and innovative African-Americans in the arts, sports, politics, music, medicine, etc.

East St. Louis, Illinois is a hell of a unique city.

Reginald Petty

LEGENDARY EAST ST LOUISANS
CONTENTS

Names with asterisks* are African American East St. Louisans who appear within the text, but are not featured.

ACKNOWLEDGMENTS

First, we would like to thank Dr. Redmond and Father Brown for offering their time and thoughtful suggestions on this text. We would also like to thank Zita Casey for lending a proofreading eye and offering helpful suggestions. *The Ebony Tree,* written by Mrs. Clementine Reeves-Hamilton and compiled by members of Delta Sigma Theta Sorority, was instrumental in helping to identify many of the early pioneers in the African American community in East St. Louis. Thank you to Charmaine Savage, Founder of *I Am East St. Louis, The Magazine*, for allowing us to use pictures from the magazine, supporting this effort with free advertising space, and offering great information.

Thank you to photographers, Stephen Bennett and Kevin Hopkins at *I Am East St. Louis, The Magazine.* Photographer Ricky Slaughter of Memories 4 U, thank you for lending free photos to this text. Thank you to JaNerra Carson for lending us the book *East St. Louis: The Way It Is* which belonged to her father, Wally Carson, a Legendary East St. Louisan also. Thank you to Dr. Stephanie Carpenter for helpful suggestions of relevant texts to use for research.

And thank you to the many East St. Louisans who offered eager suggestions of research materials.

Horace A. Adams

Photo Credit: Ebony Tree

Political Leader and Activist

A blow to the Republican Party in the City of East Saint Louis was delivered by none other than one of its great African-American leaders, Horace A. Adams. Given the current party affiliation of African- Americans, it can be hard to believe that at one time most African-Americans were Republican; however, in the early 1900's, we were devout supporters of the party of Abraham Lincoln[1], our great Illinoisan President who freed the slaves. Nevertheless, our ties to this party became strained as leaders in the African-American community in East St. Louis noticed that their fellow Republicans had come to expect the Black vote; yet, party leaders refused to serve its Black constituents, even ousting the beloved Benjamin F. Bowles from his position as Principal of Lincoln School when he refused to tow the party line.

As frustrations built in the city between Black and White Republicans, Horace A. Adams stepped forward as a leader in the Black community to fight for the rights of African-Americans in East St. Louis. Having been falsely jailed for perjury, due largely to his standing up against the Republican Party, Adams knew that he could no longer make a difference within the Republican Party and that African-Americans would be best served by leaving the party. Therefore, Adams founded the Paramount Democratic Organization (PDO), an independent party which worked with the local Democratic Party. The two parties' primary goal was identical– end the tyrannical reign of the Republican Party in East St. Louis.

Throughout the late 1920's, Adams, a natural leader and great orator, used his voice to rally against racism and to fight for the rights of his fellow Black man. Support for the PDO grew and spilled over the boundaries of East St. Louis, as the organization flourished throughout southern Illinois. In 1928, African-Americans throughout the state came out in droves to support the Democratic Party. The Democrats' statewide success was largely due to Adams who had delivered the African American vote, not only in East St. Louis, but throughout southern Illinois.

He was a forward thinker who ushered many Blacks into the Democratic Party years before other African-Americans throughout the country would cast their ballots for Democrats. He recognized the power of the Black vote, and this forethought and tenacity would lead to both extraordinary and perilous moments in his life. In 1932, Adams succeeded in having Dr. Aubrey Smith, an African American dentist from East St. Louis, placed on the ballot against fellow Democrats for the position of Illinois State Representative. Though the population of East St. Louis was mostly White, Dr. Smith won and became the first Black Illinois State Representative from the city. This extraordinary moment led Democratic leaders to order that Adams be beaten. Because of his audacity to have the Black voice heard, he was nearly killed. However, he recovered, and the success of the Paramount Democratic Organization led to the election of more African-Americans.

Unfortunately, this bright light, a beacon to his community was extinguished in a car accident. His work continued on though, as the PDO continued throughout Southern Illinois. This trailblazer was the father of three sets of twins, one of which is Dr. Lillian Parks, and one son with his wife, Edna Adams.

H.A. Adams was a noble leader and distinguished speaker who used his voice to assure that the voice of a community was heard. He is also the grandfather to the former Mayor of East St. Louis, Alvin Parks, and a Legendary East St. Louisan. [2]

Dr. Diane Bolden-Taylor

Photo Credit: Unco.edu

Opera Singer, Educator

A native East St. Louisan, Dr. Diane Bolden-Taylor was first introduced to opera while home in East St. Louis listening to a radio broadcast of "Carmen" being performed by the Metropolitan Opera. In fact, she began her singing career at her church home, Mount Zion Missionary Baptist Church.[3] After living and performing in Europe for ten years, she came home to perform for the church's Christmas concert. In an interview conducted by the Belleville News-Democrat, she said of the church, "They were my first audience, they listened to me play the piano when I couldn't play the piano; and they listened to me sing when I really don't think I knew what I was doing. But they were always in my corner."[4]

Bolden-Taylor knew that she wanted to pursue a vocal career. She received an undergraduate degree from Millikin University and a Master's Degree in Vocal Performance at Indiana University. She would go on to complete her Doctorate of Musical Arts at the University of Texas at Austin.[5] After completing her degrees at Millikin and Indiana University, Bolden-Taylor would decide that her love for the field could not be relegated to teaching only. She was not ready yet to teach vocals, she wanted to travel Europe to sing for opera agents and hopefully begin her singing career. She stated, "I had a long talk with my father and he said, 'You know, you have nothing to lose. If things don't work out, you just come back home and get a teaching job. No big deal.' I think my mother would have preferred if I had taken the more secure route, but once I made my decision, she was with me 100 percent, too."[6]

Any worries would be assuaged. She would set out on a successful 17-year career in Europe, where 'she performed with several major orchestras including the Vienna Philharmonic, the Berlin Philharmonic, and the symphony orchestras of Bonn and Palma di Mallorca.'

In the end, her father was right. She could always teach. She is now Professor Diane Bolden-Taylor. She is head of Voice Area at the University of Northern Colorado. She specializes in classical singing, voice teaching and performing art songs of European composers, as well as those of African American composers.[7] She also teaches foreign language diction.

Dr. Diane Bolden-Taylor is a world-renowned opera singer known for her beautiful lyric soprano, a professor, a winner of the Chicago Central Regional Metropolitan Opera auditions and a Legendary East St. Louisan.

Professor Benjamin F. Bowles

Educator and Activist

Professor Benjamin F. Bowles, though not born in East. St. Louis, had an indelible impact on the education of African-Americans in East St. Louis.   He began teaching at the age of 16 and continued his pedagogical service from that point on. As an emerging educator, he became well-versed in all facets of education. He had been noted as a successful music teacher, grammar school teacher, college assistant, grammar school principal and high school principal.

As a young educator in the city, he sought to provide greater educational opportunities for African-Americans. In 1900, due to his long-standing reputation as an educational leader, Professor

B.F. Bowles was appointed as the third and longest serving principal (to that point) of Lincoln School. He served the school for 14 years. During his leadership, the school thrived. He was successful in not only bolstering the educational curriculum, but also the artistic endeavors of the school. He developed the school's Art Department, thus, allowing for School Theater productions; and he developed the music department referred to in a 1903 East St. Louis Directory as being, "Especially excellent; The vocal music rendered at the commencement exercises of the Lincoln School is unsurpassed for melody and artistic rendering. Prof. Bowles has certainly succeeded in making Lincoln School a model institution." [8]

He was a leader in the political landscape of the city as a prominent member of The NAACP, and a proponent of the rights of African-Americans and African American veterans.[9]

Bowles was widowed early in his service to the community. His young wife, Annie (Anderson) Bowles died just four years into their marriage leaving him to raise their three young children. In 1902, Bowles married Carrie K. Johnson, a young teacher who would blaze her own path in the history of East St. Louis.

Professor Benjamin Bowles and wife Carrie K. Bowles were educators on the forefront of civil rights and Legendary East St. Louisans.

Carrie K. (Johnson) Bowles

Educator, Trained Social Worker, Suffragist

After teaching young students in several states, Carrie Johnson, the young educator from Ohio, decided to make her home in the burgeoning town of East St. Louis. Her educational career flourished in the city as she became a successful teacher at Lincoln School. In 1902, she would marry Professor Benjamin F. Bowles, and become step-mother to three young children. However, her new positions as an educator, wife and mother would not prove to hinder her further pursuits. According to *Groping Towards Democracy: African American Social Welfare Reform in St. Louis*, Bowles became one of the first professionally trained African American Social Workers in the Metropolitan area.[10] She was in the first class of African-American graduates of Provident School of Social Welfare. She was also a member of The League of Women Voters of St. Louis, with famed suffragist Edna Gellhorn, who was at the forefront of the fight for women's suffrage rights.

She became a community leader. As a Red Cross Volunteer and a professionally trained Social Worker with the Provost Association, the city's first large social welfare association, Carrie Bowles aided thousands of her fellow East St. Louisans who were forced to flee their homes during the race riots of 1917. She was instrumental in helping those in need after what is often considered to be one of the deadliest riots in United States History.

Professor Benjamin Bowles and wife Carrie K. Bowles were educators on the forefront of civil rights and Legendary East St. Louisans.

Father Joseph A. Brown

Jesuit Priest, Scholar, Poet

Oftentimes a story of triumph is seen only through the lens of constant ascension, but this can be misleading, especially for those who would want to follow in the footsteps of greatness. What must be understood is that those who would aspire to do something different, those who would aspire to not only break the mold, but to create a new mold, regularly suffer devastating setbacks; such is the case of Father Joseph A. Brown. His achievements are innumerable, one of the first African-American students in a Catholic School in East St. Louis, only Black student at the seminary he attended, and an Ivy League education. However, his story is a sobering look at how, when you have reached the

REGINALD PETTY and TIFFANY LEE

mountain peak, the only road forward is down into the valley; but that does not mean that the battle is over because the valley can only go so low before you find that next mountain to climb. Father Brown's story exemplifies that greatness is found only by continuing to conquer the mountain that stares down boldly in front of you.

Joseph Brown is a native of East St. Louis and was one of the first African American students to attend Catholic schools in the city. His path to ordination would start in high school, during a visit by a priest from Notre Dame University. Brown's conversation with the priest about wanting to be a teacher, would lead to a recommendation by his principal to a Jesuit Seminary, and ultimately his acceptance into said seminary. Jesuits are an order of priests whose focus is on education and teaching. The current leader of the Catholic Church, Pope Francis, is a Jesuit. They believe in critical thinking and excellence in education. Father Brown would attend the Jesuit school as the first African American student. The intense pressure associated with being the first; and the face and figure of change caused a mental breakdown. He says, "I was trying my best to absorb all kinds of ignorance and confusion, and I was trying to be somebody who could bridge the gaps, who could just be all things to all people. No 18-, 19- or 20-year-old should have to do that, especially when I had no support system." This breakdown would not stop him though, he would recover and become the first African American Jesuit Priest from East St. Louis.

His further education would focus on several of his interests. He would receive his Bachelor's from St. Louis University in Philosophy, an M.A. in Writing Seminars from Johns Hopkins University, and three degrees from Yale University: M.A. in Afro-American Studies, M.A. in American Studies and a Ph.D. in American Studies. Creative Arts have always interested Father Brown, in fact he would say that immersion in Creative Arts and educating himself on African American culture would aid in his recovery while in seminary school. As a writer, he became a published author in high school. He has continued to publish hundreds of works, including books, poems, essays, pamphlets, learning materials and pictorials. His works often focus on the intersection of race, religion, and creativity; case in point, his first published book, *Accidental Grace*, which is a book of poetry published in the oft-celebrated, "Callaloo Series" which publishes African Diaspora Arts. Another example is a collection which Brown coauthored entitled, *Where Were You? A Meditation on Lynching*; this work is a presentation which includes pictures, literature and gospel music. The 25 pictures included in the presentation are postcards collected by James Allen, which display people who were mutilated and lynched. People would send these postcards to each other by U.S. mail just as people might send a postcard today to say, "Hi, from Chicago." His thoughts on the work are published in an article from 2002. "Brown said for 200 years of American history, lynching was one of the preferred methods of social control, and possibly one of the greatest examples of domestic terrorism ever on the planet. He said there is evidence the motivations that fueled the brutal murders of the past can still be found in American society today."

Brown is not only a great artist, and religious leader, but he also became the teacher that he always wanted to be. After serving for sixteen years as either Director of the Black American Studies Program or Chair of Southern Illinois University at Carbondale's (SIUC) Africana Studies and Director of Black American Studies. Brown is now a full-time professor in his department. His road here would also be marred by what might have been perceived as defeats. After teaching at some of the best universities in the country, Creighton, Xavier, and the University of Virginia, he was fired due to office politics and his reputation was tarnished. He describes the experience, "It was a very painful moment in my life. It was probably one of the most devastating things I ever went through." However, he turned to writing and published more works. Years later, he would see a job opening at SIUC, and though Ivy League educated, well published and with teaching credentials from the best schools in the country, he was not the first choice of the school, and was hired only when another candidate 'didn't work out.' Since teaching at SIUC, Father Brown has changed a fledgling minor in Black Studies to a major and created a department devoted to the study. He says, "I came here with my own game plan to build the program so it could become a major with as much academic respect and integrity as any other. I found intense university opposition to that, but I pushed on, hired faculty, hired administrative staff and taught every kind of class I could imagine so we'd have classes on the books that would be broad enough to be the foundation of a major." And though he has accomplished so much, the humility of a man who looks at the program that he founded at SIUC, as a work in progress, who focuses just as much on his failures as his successes in an interview that was slated to highlight his accomplishments, shows the quiet greatness often not sensationalized in movies or books. It is, however, a story that should be told because it is a raw reality check of what it takes to be great.

(Dr.) Father Joseph A. Brown is a Legendary East St. Louisan.

William Washington Buchanan Jr.

Served the East St. Louis Community for over 60 years.

In 1937, a small pharmacy was opened in the African American section of East St. Louis. It was not a major milestone; as it was not the first African American pharmacy, Haynes Pharmacy had been opened in 1915 on 19th and Bond Ave.[11] It would be one of many African American pharmacies in the city, as later Richard Levelle Sykes would open two separate pharmacies also. What stands out more about South End Pharmacy, was that it was the last African American pharmacy in the city of East St. Louis.

William Washington Buchanan Jr. was born in East St. Louis; the eldest son of William Washington Buchanan Sr. The elder Buchanan was a soldier in the Spanish-American War and was a trombonist with the famed "Eighth Illinois Band." The elder Buchanan was a custodian and messenger for Southern Illinois National Bank. As a child, Buchanan often visited Haynes drugstore for snacks. He says, in an article in the St. Louis Post-Dispatch, that Haynes is where he got a spark.[12] He liked the idea of being hands-on with people and actively helping them to feel better. Therefore, after graduating from Lincoln High School, he would go to the University of Illinois at Chicago, Pharmacy School. He was the lone African American student in the Class of

93 students. After graduating, he would go to the University of Illinois, Urbana-Champaign, to earn a Master's Degree in Biology. Here, he would meet his wife Geneva, also from East St. Louis, and they would return to the city together to open their business. By day, they ran South End Pharmacy and by night they lived in an apartment in the back of the business.

In 1940, he would move just across the street from his original location. His father had helped him secure a loan from his employer, Southern Illinois National Bank, to build a pharmacy at 1652 Central Ave. During the interview with the reporter from St. Louis Post-Dispatch, 67 years after receiving the loan, Buchanan still bristled at the fact that his father, though entrusted as a messenger for the bank with transferring millions of dollars, was only able to receive the bank loan by offering his life insurance policy as collateral. The new South End Pharmacy was built with several doctors' offices in the rear. South End Pharmacy was a bustling business. In the city, people patronized their local African American businesses, and they flourished. Not only was the pharmacy a one stop shop for all of the community's healthcare needs, but it was a social spot, where teens would come for ice cream and floats. They would sit and enjoy their goodies at the counter. In its early days, Buchanan would have delivery boys who would delivered prescriptions by bicycle. As the business grew, deliveries were being made in a Model T. Buchanan would have his daughter, Betty Buchanan, also a pharmacist, to fill-in for him when he couldn't make it to work.

REGINALD PETTY and TIFFANY LEE

In 2005, it was no longer a bustling business, and Buchanan was no longer an eager man in his 20's. He was a 92-year-old who showed up to work to serve a community that he had served for 65 years. He had held on to his pharmacy license, but customers no longer came there to have prescriptions filled. They had moved on to the big box stores – Walgreens and Walmart. The doctors' offices had closed too. The last one in 2004. When asked about the customers, Buchanan said that they had either moved or died– but South End Pharmacy had stayed. The elder Buchanan had long ago passed. His brother, famed Lincoln High School band leader, Elwood Buchanan who had instructed Miles Davis, Willie Walker, Frank Gully,[13] and many more musicians who would become famous, had passed also. However, through losing customers who were no longer relegated to the South End of the city or even the city at all; through losing customers who no longer felt a connection to their locally owned African American businesses; through three robberies at gunpoint; South End Pharmacy had stayed. By 2005, the business was only a confectionary of sorts that sold candy and snacks; however, Buchanan had stayed to become the lone African American pharmacy in the city of East St. Louis. There are no awards for being the last, but maybe there should be an honor for those who stay – for those who spend a lifetime serving one city. At the age of 99, William Washington Buchanan Jr. passed without much fanfare, but his dedication must be remembered.

William Washington Buchanan Jr. is a Legendary East St. Louisan.

Dwight Bush Sr.

The United States Ambassador to Morocco

Dwight Bush Sr. is a proud native of East St. Louis.[14] During his Senate confirmation hearings, he described East St. Louis as "a town of rich history whose boom and bust cycles reflect both the hope and tragedy of industrial America."[15]

After graduating from East St. Louis Sr. High, he would go on to earn his B.A. in Government and Economics at Cornell University. Soon after graduating, he began climbing the rungs of the corporate ladder by starting as a trainee in the management development program at Chase Manhattan Bank.[16] His distinguished 15-year career at Chase would have him traveling to

Latin America, the Middle East, and Asia for corporate banking assignments. It would also result in him becoming the first African American managing director of Chase.

In 1994, he would leave Chase Bank, and join Sallie Mae Corporation, serving as vice president of corporate development until 1997. This would lead to continued growth in his career; from 1998 to 2006; Bush worked as a principal at Stuart Mill Capital, LLC; vice president and chief financial officer at Sato Travel Holdings, Inc.; and vice chairman of Enhanced Capital Partners, LLC.

In 2002, he decided to form his own business. Bush established D. L. Bush & Associates, a Washington, DC-based financial advisory and business consulting firm. In 2004, he also founded Urban Trust Bank. Before leaving in 2008, he was president and CEO of Urban Trust Bank, Urban Trust Holdings and president of UTB Education Finance, LLC. He also worked as vice chairman and director of Entre Med, Inc.

Although already highly successful, Bush's career would go on to reach even greater heights. On August 1, 2013, Bush was nominated by President Barack Obama to serve as the United States Ambassador to Morocco. During his hearings he would speak kindly of East St Louis saying that he was "fortunate to have grown up with the working class families, the great teachers, and the mentors that helped [him] along the way." In March of 2014, the United States Senate confirmed his appointment. Thus, he is currently serving as the United States Ambassador to Morocco.[17]

Dwight Bush Sr. is an impressive businessman, an entrepreneur, a United States Ambassador, and a Legendary East St. Louisan.

Leo Chears

The Man in the Red Vest

Legendary East St. Louisan, Leo Chairs, was a transplant to the town. He was born in Lamar, Mississippi, but his family moved North when he was eight to Brooklyn; however, two years later the family would decide to make East St. Louis their home.

Mr. Chears served his country, married the love of his life, Betty Jo Stewart, and started a family, all before he found the second love of his life, broadcasting. In 1962, Chears began a career in broadcasting that would span over four decades.[18] His broadcasting career began at the East St. Louis station WBBR, which was later renamed WAMV and would still later be renamed to the call letters WESL.

During Chears career, radio was a popular medium for the African American community; however, at that time, radio was still segregated. Though 'Black' music was growing in popularity with both White and Black audiences, there was still a racial divide. Many African American broadcasters were relegated to **AM** only 'Black' stations, and even these stations were generally owned by Caucasian men.[19] So it was a testament to his dedication and talent that by the end of 1962 he had gained a job at KADI-**FM** in St. Louis.

Chears would later work at several local radio stations including KSD, WRTH and WSIE. Many radio stations were changing formatting to R&B or Rock & Roll to accommodate the masses, but Leo Chears was the 'Jazz Man,' and refused to cater to 'popular music trends.' In a 1995 interview with Doug Kaufman of the *Belleville News-Democrat,* Chears stated, "I play jazz as a culture. Whether it's Stan Kenton or Miles (Davis) or (John) Coltrane or whomever, it's the way I feel like it ought to be."

Not only would Chears play Jazz, but he would interview jazz greats on his show such as: Dizzie Gillespie, Joe Williams, Jimmy Smith, Gene Ammons, Arthur Prysock, and Billy Eckstine to name a few, according to his obituary in *The Monitor.* His radio shows were always supplemented by his own collection which included a greater variety and selection of music than that owned by the radio stations. His opinions on jazz were respected, as he grew to become THE authority on jazz in the metropolitan area. In his column for *The East St. Louis Monitor*, "The Cat Bird Seat," he would sometimes review shows or works by artists. His writing echoed his smooth broadcasting approach as can be seen in this excerpt from his column on February 23, 1967:

> "JAZZ came to East St. Louis this past SUNDAY and found the people of this METRO-AREA—READY –and WILLING…it came on the horns – drums – vibes – organs – piano's and Bass's of some of the greatest local talent ever put in one place together…."

Because of his popularity, he became a spokesperson for Anheuser-Busch which would lead to his tag, "Man in the Red Vest." Chears would wear his red vest to connect with the signature color red of Anheuser-Busch. Chears would continue broadcasting his jazz show until December 18, 2005, shortly before his death on January 6, 2006.

Due to his contributions to radio, he was inducted into the St. Louis Radio Hall of Fame as a Legacy Member. His tradition of sharing jazz with the metro area continues on as his child, Terri Chears-Long, donated a portion of his collection to the Lovejoy Library at Southern Illinois University at Edwardsville. This donation included 500 jazz music cds, 250 selected jazz LP albums, and reel-to-reel tapes of recorded interviews conducted by Leo Chears of some of the greatest musicians in the world. [20]

Leo Chears, 'The Man in the Red Vest,' jazz authority, St. Louis Radio Hall of Famer, and Legendary East St. Louisan.

Bryon Cox

Photo Credit: *I Am EStl The Magazine*, Stephen Bennett

Cox Would Leave for College a Star and Come Back Even Greater

For almost four decades, Brian Cox has been a part of the game of football. He began playing football at Wilson Elementary in East St. Louis and is currently the Atlanta Falcons' line coach.[21] As a young kid growing up in East St. Louis, he played several sports including football, baseball and basketball. In high school, he would play under Coach Bob Shannon, a legendary coach who won several titles with East St. Louis High School – about whom a book was pinned, *The Right Kind of Heroes.*

Cox would leave East St. Louis a star– an undefeated state and national champion, then go on to Western Illinois University on a scholarship.[22] Even with all of his successes, he would struggle in college and consider quitting; however, his mother made him stay the course, and he would graduate with a degree in Mass Communication, and as a standout in football. In his senior year at Western, in 1990, Cox was named an All-American after leading the team in tackles and interceptions and was selected as the Gateway Football Conference's Defensive Player of the Decade.[23]

When he was selected by the Miami Dolphins in the fifth round, 113th overall pick in the 1991 NFL, he would be one of the select few of college athletes who make it into the NFL.[24] As a professional football player, Cox would also be a standout, playing 12 seasons in the NFL. He would retire in 2002, as a winner of a Super Bowl, a three-time Pro Bowl selectee, and having posted over 51sacks.[25] After retiring from the league, he would use his Mass Communications Degree, as an analyst for TVG Network.

In 2006, he would begin a coveted career with the New York Jets, as an assistant defensive coach. He continued to build his career as a successful coach as he climbed the career ladder with teams such as the Buccaneers, Browns, and Dolphins. He is currently the defensive line coach for the Atlanta Falcons. Cox has had a career in football that many young athletes only dream about, but he has remained grounded, saying in an interview with Maurice Scott Jr. from *I Am EStL The Magazine,* "I'm just the frontman in this band. I'm James Brown. But I have a band playing behind me called family."

He continues to give back to his community; Cox and his family formed the Creating Opportunities for eXcellence (C.O.X.) Foundation, a charitable organization devoted to helping East St. Louis children with educational and athletic opportunities. The foundation has offered scholarships and guidance to many youths. In 2013, the foundation began its first Youth Football Clinic, where it offered free instruction by NFL coaches and players to children between the ages of 5-17.[26]

Bryan Cox– high school football standout, College football standout, NFL standout, NFL Coach and Legendary East St. Louisan.

Miles Dewey Davis III

Davis' Influence in Jazz Has Spanned Over Seven Decades

As a testament to his ingenious creativity, immense talent and multigenerational influence on music, *Everything's Beautiful*, a 2016 posthumous release of works by Miles Davis would break records and enter the Billboard 200 list.[27] Davis, considered the greatest influence on not only jazz, but music in his era, was born in 1926 and is the son of a respected dentist and an English teacher. Davis was given his first trumpet at the age of 13, by his East St. Louis neighbor, Dr. Eubanks. He was influenced early on by Elwood Buchanan, another East St. Louisan, whose band produced several notable musicians – Willie Walker, Frank Gully, Red Bonner and many others.[28] Buchanan was known for emphasizing playing the trumpet without bravado. Davis would integrate this playing style into his own form.

His talents would send him from Lincoln High School to Julliard, to the top of the charts, to being the most prominent Jazz musician in history. While still in high school, Davis is said to have played with Charlie Parker, the pioneer of bebop. He was a stand-in for a sick trumpet player in Parker's band.[29] Thus, upon arriving in New York for Julliard, Davis would join the band of Charlie Parker, his idol.[30] The two would play at Harlem

Nightclubs, and Davis would regularly collaborate with several musicians that he met during this time, helping to further define bebop– a fast, instrumental jazz pioneered by Charlie Parker. His style would focus heavily on improvisation– allowing the mood and the music to guide his playing. Davis recorded frequently with Parker in the mid-40's, as a member of Parker's Quintet.

Then, as a bandleader, he would form several different groups, often of great musicians who would go on to be prominent in jazz as well, such as John Coltrane, Paul Chambers, Wayne Shorter, Tony Williams, Ron Carter and many others. Over the years, his style would change; and when Davis changed, jazz changed. From bebop, to hard-bop, to 'cool jazz' to jazz fusion, to experimentation with instruments never used in jazz, Davis kept the jazz audience wanting more. Davis struggled with drug addiction at different points in his life, and though his performances suffered, he would continue to work; therefore, his absence from 1975 to 1981 due to alcohol and drug abuse left a void in the music scene. However, in 1981, he would reenter music with interpretations of popular pop songs of the age, and then in 1986, he would again reinvent himself.

From *Birth of Cool* in the 1940's to Grammy Award winner 'Aura' released in 1989, Davis would reinvent his style, and therefore Jazz 'five or six times.' He is a nine-time Grammy Award-winning artist, and a recipient of the Lifetime Achievement Grammy Award. With the release of *Everything's Beautiful* in

May 2016, it must be noted that Davis' influence in jazz has spanned over seven decades.

Miles Davis– the Prince of Darkness,[31] the Creator of 'Cool' is a Legendary East St. Louisan.

Katherine Dunham

A World Renowned Ethnographer, Entertainer, Activist, and Scholar

Though born in Chicago, in 1909, Katherine Dunham chose East St. Louis as her home in 1967. The mayor at the time of her death, Carl Officer, spoke the sentiments of a city during a program given to commemorate her life, "It is indeed an honor to be the mayor of a city that Katherine Dunham chose to live in. She could have lived anywhere in the world, but she chose East St. Louis."[32] Though trained in ballet, and known for her acting, beauty and choreography which helped to launch African American Dance onto a national and international art stage, Katherine Dunham was also a scholar, who was one of the first African American women who studied at the prestigious

University of Chicago. She earned a Bachelors, Masters and Doctoral Degree in Anthropology from the school.[33]

Dunham had long loved dancing and singing, and began performing gospel as a young child. Therefore, she took dance classes while in college and created the Negro Dance Group. The group performed in many places, including with the Chicago Opera Company. Dunham was also invited to perform in front of the Rosenwald Foundation, this performance would prove to be the impetus to the fusion of her two loves– anthropology and dance. Because of her beautiful performance, the Rosenfeld Foundation offered her an endowment to study dance. Using the endowment, she would travel the world to study dance. She would go on to study ritualistic dancing in Trinidad, Haiti, Jamaica, and throughout the Caribbean. Her study in the area would lead to a new educational discipline, Dance Anthropology. In an interview, she said that dance was more than just about personal pleasure, it was about "Expressing your culture, expressing the meaning of your life, the meaning of the people that you came from, the meaning of your family, and your roots, ...dance does this. It's in there, we just have to take it out and use it."

A cultural anthropologist, known as the Matriarch of Black Dance, the first African-American to choreograph for the Metropolitan Opera, author of several works, actor in over a dozen Hollywood movies, a performer in over 57 countries throughout the world, Katherine Dunham chose East St. Louis. Before her arrival, the city had begun in a downward spiral; this is what led her to East St. Louis. She decided to dedicate her craft, her image, her knowledge to help save the people of the city. She created The Performing Arts Training Center and the Dunham Dynamic Museum in an effort to redirect the energy of Black youth away from the violence of hopelessness towards the pride gained through performing dances created by their ancestors.

She dedicated years to the city and to the tireless fight of racial and socioeconomic injustices throughout the world. Because of her dedication to the promotion of and acceptance of African traditions and African American Culture, she stands as one of the most important figures of the 20th Century. Although a decade has passed since her death, tributes in her honor continue each year. Dunham Technique Classes are still offered by universities.

For her dedication, she has received many awards including an Honorary Degree in Fine Arts from Harvard University, the Presidential Medal of Arts, Kennedy Center Honors, the plaque d'Honneur Haitian-American Chamber of Commerce Award, the French Legion of Honor, the Southern Cross of Brazil, Grand Cross of Haiti, the NAACP Lifetime Achievement Award, The Albert Schweitzer Music Award at Carnegie Hall, the Lincoln Academy Laureate, and the Urban Leagues' Lifetime Achievement Award.

Katherine Dunham is a world-renowned ethnographer, entertainer, activist, scholar, and a Legendary East St. Louisan.

Dr. Harry Edwards

Photo Credit: I Am EStL, The Magazine/ Stephen Bennett

A Legend in Sports, a Legend in the Civil Rights Movement, a Legend in Academia

Atop an Olympic victory podium, two young, Black men stand; shoeless, heads hung, with black-gloved, fisted hands raised to the sky– in solidarity with the Civil Rights Movement, and in defiance of an America who would in 1968 hold itself as the leader of the 'free' world while still denying African-Americans the tenets promised in the Declaration of Independence almost 200 years before, that "…all men are created equal, that they are endowed by their Creator with certain unalienable Rights, that among these are Life, Liberty and the pursuit of Happiness." This defiant act, which sought to expose America's hypocrisy on a worldwide stage was orchestrated by the Olympic Movement for Human Rights. Its leader was none other than native East St. Louisan, Dr. Harry Edwards.[34]

Dr. Henry Edwards was one, in a family of eight children, being raised by a single father with a third-grade education who emphasized athletics as the way to escape the constraints of poverty.[35] Edwards, a standout in basketball and track, graduated from East St. Louis High and went to Fresno City College on a basketball and track scholarship. He would then go on to San Jose State University. Although an exceptional athlete, even setting a record in the discus throw, Edwards was dismissed from the team for voicing his concerns about the unequal treatment of African-American athletes as compared to their Caucasian counterparts.[36] Upon graduation from San Jose State University, Edwards chose not to pursue a career in professional sports– instead he chose academia. He would go to Cornell University for his Master's in Sociology; then, return to his undergraduate alma mater, San Jose State University as a part-time sociology instructor.

The Olympic Black Power salutes would be the crescendo of a resistance launched on the San Jose State University campus, which would result in the firing of Edwards; and the dismissing of Thomas Smith and John Carlos (the athletes on the Olympic stand), from the Olympic team. Even though they had won the Gold (Smith) and Bronze (Carlos) medals, their resistance had cost them their spots on the Olympic Team. Standing up to make a difference, Edwards emphasizes, will cost you. All men became infamous for the act. Edwards was the subject of FBI surveillance. Edwards work with the Olympic Movement for Human Rights can also be seen on ESPN's *OJ: Made in America*.[37]

Upon losing his job, Edwards would return to Cornell for his PhD in Sociology and later become a leader in the field of Sports Sociology. In an interview with Cal Sports in 1999, he stated of his experience, "What people failed to see was that society reverberates through sports and vice versa." In the 60's, people assumed that because athletes were allowed to play on a professional or collegiate sports team, that they were being treated equally. Edwards, Smith, Carlos, along with other notable athletic figures – Muhammad Ali, and Kareem Abdul-Jabbar challenged the presupposition that access and equality were one and the same.

After earning his PhD, he would go on to teach at the University of California, Berkley, in 1971.[38] He would become a tenured professor at the University. He is still a highly sought-after lecturer and has written four books– *Black Student* (1970); *Revolt of The Black Athlete* (1970), *Healing Intelligence* (1971) and *The Struggle That Must Be* (1980). His expertise in the fields of sports, sociology and race would lead him to work with major league baseball, the San Francisco Forty-Niners, the Golden State Warriors, the NFL and several universities on equality in sports. He would work with the teams on many concerns including– overcoming racial issues between team members and racial disparities in representation of minorities in upper administration.

According to an article in *I Am East St. Louis,* Edwards was recruited by NFL Coach Bill Walsh in 1986. His input led to the 1992 adoption by the NFL of a Minority Coaches Internship Program; and implementations of programs such as "the college degree completion program, post career occupational prep program with internships; finance and tax advice programs; and personal and family counseling."[39]

On May 28, 2016, Edwards delivered the commencement address and was given an honorary Doctorate of Humane Letters by San Jose State University, the same university that had branded him as a radical and fired him in the 60's had decided to honor his storied career.

Dr. Harry Edwards is a legend in sports, a legend in the Civil Rights Movement, a legend in academia, and a Legendary East St. Louisan.

Dr. John Eubanks Jr.

Photo Credit: Ebony Tree

A Political Activist and Respected Physician

Dr. John Eubanks Jr. was a native of East St. Louis born on August 28, 1896, to John Eubanks Sr. and Belle Eubanks. His father, John Eubanks Sr., had an indelible impact on the city. He was a police officer during the 1917 riots and helped African American families fleeing the city to cross the Free Bridge,[40] though African American police officers were told by their superiors to stay home during the riots. He was one of the few[41]wh o disobeyed the orders and helped to save the lives of other African-Americans.[42]

His son, John Eubanks Jr., would also prove to be a valuable citizen of East St. Louis; however, his service would be in a different capacity, as a Physician. After graduating from Lincoln High School, he would enter Howard University for pre-med training.[43] According to the *Ebony Tree,* Eubanks education was interrupted as he was called to serve overseas in World War I. While in the military, he attended U.S. Army Intelligence School.[44] He was injured during the war and discharged as a disabled veteran. He would complete his undergraduate studies at Howard, and complete his medical degree at the University of Illinois, College of Medicine.

After graduating from school, he came back to East St. Louis and established a medical practice. The Eubanks name was well respected in the community as he was knowledgeable and very kind. Miles Davis, in his autobiography, says that Eubanks bought him his first trumpet. Beyond this fascinating point, he was an integral part of the community. Besides his medical practice, he donated his time to civic organizations. He was a member of the NAACP and later would become president of NAACP. He was the leader of the NAACP's Well-Baby Clinic. He was also a member of the St. Clair County Republican League, an African American political group devoted to increasing the quality of life of African American constituents within the city through political action.

Dr. John Eubanks, a political activist, a respected physician and a Legendary East St. Louisan.

Dr. Larry Gladney

His Accomplishments are 'Out of this World'

Dr. Larry Gladney, Research Physicist, Professor, and author or coauthor of over 600 published scholarly articles on physics is an East St. Louisan. As a baby, Gladney moved to East St. Louis with his mother, Annie Lee Gladney. His mother was a sharecropper. She was an important influence in his life, and also had a love for science. He says in an interview on thehistorymakers.com[45] that most of the science that he had encountered, chemistry and biology, were not the kind of science that he found interesting. His calling came when he was just 13,

47

after discovering a book on physics in his Clark Jr. High School's library. Though still young and just learning about the field, he knew he was hooked.

By high school he "had already been set on the path to becoming a physicist." So in 1975, after graduating third in his class at East St. Louis High School, he went on to study physics at Northwestern, and later received his Master's and Ph.D. from Stanford University. His expertise is in experimental high energy physics and cosmology.

Currently, Dr. Gladney teaches at the University of Pennsylvania, where he has served as the Physics Department Chair. He is now the Associate Dean for Natural Sciences; as such, he oversees the Departments of Biology, Chemistry, Earth and Environmental Science, Linguistics, Mathematics, Physics and Astronomy, and Psychology, as well as several research centers. He has made immeasurable contributions to the field of Physics due to the wealth of information included in his published works alone. However, he continues his research activities and was the co-leader for the Supernova/Acceleration Probe (SNAP) simulation team, which is a proposed space observatory designed to measure the expansion of the universe and to determine the nature of the mysterious Dark Energy that is accelerating this expansion. SNAP is a joint venture between NASA and the United States Department of Energy.

For his contributions to the field, he was awarded the Edward A. Bouchet Award from the American Physical Society – awarded only once a year to a distinguished minority physicist who has made significant contributions to physics research. Wayne State University awarded him the Martin Luther King Jr. Lecturer Award.[46] Because of his work with minorities and youths, he was the recipient of the Outstanding Community Service Award from the Penn Black Graduate Professional Students Association. Furthermore, he was awarded the Edmund J. and Louise W. Kahn Chair for Faculty Excellence.

He is a sought after lecturer and researcher, and has developed numerous courses at the University of Pennsylvania.

Dr. Gladney, Physicist, Scholar, and a Legendary East St. Louisan.

Archie Dewey Grimmett

Patriot, Fighting for the Rights of His Fellow Man

Upon graduating from Southern Illinois University at
Carbondale, Archie Grimmett would decide to enlist in the U.S.
Air Force. This would launch his career of service to the United
States. After four years, he was honorably discharged, and began
employment as a GS-2[47] with the U.S. Securities and Exchange
Commission in Washington D.C. Though he started as one of the
lowest ranking civilian employees in 1962, he would quickly prove
himself valuable to the United States Government by serving in
several different capacities with the United States Postal Service
and the Department of the Army. By 1968, his career had
flourished. He served on the United States Commission on Civil

Rights, and in 1969, he became the first African American Personnel Director for the Commission. He would serve in this position until 1972.

In 1972, he would begin working at the Smithsonian. His platform at the Smithsonian was about inclusion. Thus, he would establish their first Office of Equal Opportunity. Through this office, he promoted increased representation of African-Americans in Smithsonian exhibits and increased employment of women and minorities. He would go on to become the Director of the Office of Equal Opportunity and be promoted to GS-15, the highest civilian rank.

He would later serve as the Chief of Civilian Personnel at the Pentagon for the Department of the Army. Here he would implement a successful interchange employment program between the ROTC and Army commands. He was Personnel Director for the United States Army Material Command headquarters and later Director of Civilian Personnel for the U.S. Army (USAREUR) in Germany. In this position, he represented the U.S. government in all civilian employment matters where the U.S. Army was the chief employer, including negotiating with host governments, and the Status of Forces Agreements affecting local and national employment.

After 36 years, Archie Grimmett retired from his storied career with the United States. The programs that he implemented within the government promoted inclusion of all races and both genders. He also saved the government hundreds of thousands of dollars through programs implemented to promote efficiency. His determination propelled him from a GS-2, almost the lowest ranking civilian employee, to the highest rank (GS-15) of a Civilian Employee.

Archie Grimmett is a Patriot, and as a native of this city, he is a Legendary East St. Louisan.[48]

Dr. Clifford Harper

Photo Credit: cdharperbook.com

Scholar and Writer

Only someone with an esteemed career such as the one that Dr. Clifford Harper created can retire to a career of writing successful novels. Harper, also known as CD Harper, has been a successful educator, a successful educational administrator, a successful playwright; and once he retired, he became a successful novelist.

A native East St. Louisan, Dr. Harper's life would begin as a young boy in the South End – confined like his peers, by government-sanctioned segregation. However, that would not stop him from coming home to begin his career at his alma mater,

Lincoln Sr. High. He had returned to teach the sons and daughters of the peers with whom he had walked those same halls.

As an adult, he had broken the confines of his youth, and graduated from the University of Illinois; he would get his Master's in Speech and Theatre; and go on to become one of the first African-Americans to earn a PhD in English from St. Louis University.

Dr. Harper says that his students at Lincoln, would inspire him to write plays. Though he would leave the school to further his career, his works have often harkened back to his experiences in East St. Louis. His play, "Neva's Tale," would focus on an African American family in East St. Louis who must struggle through a family curse. "Neva's Tale" was performed at Los Angeles Theatre Center to great acclaim. Another play, "Black Bridge" would focus on the race riots of 1917. He also wrote, "At All Cost," a play about George Washington and his slave, Billy Lee. Beyond his original works, he directed works by August Wilson, Lorraine Hansberry and James Baldwin.

Though already proven as a distinguished playwright, he would prove himself to be a successful educator and educational administrator. He served as Dean of the University and Provost of Fisk University.[49] He was Director of Black Studies, Associate Professor of English and Dean of General Academic Programs at Southern Illinois University at Carbondale.[50] At Cal State University, Los Angeles, he was Executive Assistant to the President, and Chair of the Department of Theatre, Arts and

Dance. As Chair of the department, he was the Founding Executive Director of the Luckman Fine Arts Complex and the Luckman Jazz Orchestra. He created the "Theatre for the 21ˢᵗ Century" and revived the Dance Kaleidoscope program. His work with Katherine Dunham, which he counts as one of his achievements, could have been inspiration for this revival.

After 30 years of serving as a playwright and educator, he decided to retire; however, retirement would be the start of a new career as a novelist. He began the trilogy *In the Beginning: The Life and Times of Liberty and Slavery* which is 'the culmination of his desire to put his thoughts and creative impulses to use in pursuit of an American History more reflective of the complexities that are this nation.'[51] Book one, *Covenant* and Book two, *And Face the Unknown* have been published and well received. Book three, *Not a Slave, Yet a Slave* is soon to be published.

Dr. Clifford Harper has so many accolades, and he can add one more title to his résumé, Legendary East St. Louisan.

Dawn Harper-Nelson

Photo Credit: Memories4U, Ricky Slaughter

Birth of a Champion

Looking at her storied career now, one can hardly imagine that at the Olympic trials in 2008, Dawn Harper-Nelson was not expected to be a contender. She had had knee surgery approximately two months before the Olympic trials in 2008, and had been working three jobs while still training for the Olympics. In an interview with the Belleville News-Democrat,[52] after qualifying for the Beijing Olympics, Harper-Nelson said, "I just told myself that there weren't a lot of people who thought that I would be here and that I just wanted to run the race I knew I was capable of running." She struggled in the trial and thought that she may not make the team, but by .007 seconds, she would make the team and earn her place in the Beijing Olympics.

With her Olympic coach Bob Kersee and Olympian Jackie Joyner-Kersee there to support her, Harper-Nelson would run the 100-meter hurdle Olympic race using someone else's shoes. At the start of the race, she smiles easily and points to the sky in recognition of God when introduced. She strides smoothly through the race, and dips forward at the end, and continues forward after the race to high-five fans in the stands, while her counterparts return to review the scoreboard. She wins Gold! With elation she turns a cartwheel and again points to the sky. Her winning bouquet would be shared with adoring fans.

She was a champion, and would go on to constantly prove herself as such with an Olympic Silver Medal in 2012. By 2015, Harper-Nelson would be a four-time Diamond League Champion. Though recognition of her talents by media outlets would be slow to come, she had always been beloved by her hometown, East St. Louis, for the champion that she had always been. At East St. Louis High School, Harper-Nelson had been a six time Illinois State title winner. The only difference in her status as a champion was ...now the world knew. She returned home to a parade in her honor.

In an interview with Fox 2 News, she said, "It means the world to me to know that East St. Louis backed me 100 percent. I really went out there to represent them and the USA.... East St. Louis needs a bright light to be shined on them, and I felt like I could be that...I always want to shine a positive light because I feel like there are great people that come from the City of Champions, East St. Louis."[53] She not only shines a light, but she gives back to the city, helping needy families and donating time and support to the Jackie Joyner-Kersee Foundation. Moreover, she is a spokesperson for the American Diabetes Association and an Ambassador for United Way of Greater St. Louis.

Always one to exceed all expectations, Harper-Nelson was preparing for her third Olympic Games, while also earning her PhD in Psychology.[54] Unfortunately, due to injury, she was unable to participate; however, she proudly covered the Olympics for NBC.

Legendary East St. Louisan Dawn Harper-Nelson is a champion amongst a "City of Champions."

Dr. Katie Harper-Wright

"Deeply ingrained within the fiber of my personal and professional philosophy is that each child is a unique and precious individual."

Dr. Katie Wright is an East St. Louisan by way of St. Louis. Wright, has spent over 70 years assuring that children receive a quality education. She has been quoted in the St. Louis American as saying, "Deeply ingrained within the fiber of my personal and professional philosophy is that each child is a unique and precious individual."[55] She, too, was a unique child, as she graduated from Vashon High School at the age of 16, and would go on to graduate from the University of Illinois in Urbana-Champaign by the time she was 20 years old. While there, she excelled, and became the first African American student to serve on the University of Illinois

Debate Team. She would later earn a Master's degree from the college also. She earned her Doctorate in Special Education and Political Science at St. Louis University.

As a teacher, Dr. Wright would begin teaching in East St. Louis School District 189. She would ascend to become the Director of Special Education for the East St. Louis Area Joint Agreement, School Districts 188/189.[56] Due to her endless work in special education, Dr. Wright was appointed by President George W. Bush to the President's Commission on Excellence in Special Education. For the district, she would serve in several capacities including – Media Director and Interim Superintendent. After retiring from teaching the youth, she would take her talents to Harris-Stowe and instruct future educators on how to properly educate children. For her work there, she would become the first, Adjunct Professor Emeritus at Harris Stowe State University.

Wright has been a torchbearer for both women and African Americans. She is a member of the Mensa Society. She was the first women to serve as assistant superintendent of East St. Louis District 189. She was the first African-American to become a member, then the first to become president of both the St. Clair County Mental Health Board and East St. Louis Library.

Dr. Wright has been a member and donated her time to several organizations. She is a member, past chapter president, past national officer of, and current Historian Emeritus for the East St. Louis Alumni Chapter of Delta Sigma Theta Sorority. She has served as National Editor for the Top Ladies of Distinction. She has also donated time to the NAACP, United Way, East St. Louis Financial Advisory Authority, the Girl Scouts of America, and the Urban League. One article is not enough to explore the life of this great woman who has received over 300 awards for her service and excellence. Even, at the tender age of 92, Wright continues her service. She was appointed by President Barack Obama to serve on the United States Selective Service Board.

Due to her contributions in education, the Dr. Katie Wright Elementary School at 7710 State Street, East St. Louis, IL was erected in her honor. Wright has fully adopted the city of East St. Louis as her own, as she continues to live in and serve the community. "Others have left, but I'm still here," she says of adopting the city. "This is home." She credits her husband and life partner, Marvin Wright with helping her to achieve her goals.

Dr. Katie Harper-Wright has led a Legendary Life, and due to her adoption of the city is also a Legendary East St. Louisan.

Eugene Haynes Jr.

Classical Pianist, The "Maestro" of East St. Louis

Eugene Haynes Jr. is a native East St. Louisan who was born in his home on Missouri Ave. This was not an uncommon practice as many African-American children were delivered by a doctor in their home due to segregation policies in the East St. Louis hospitals. Mr. Haynes was a self-taught musical prodigy whose talents became clear at the young age of four. He would build upon his natural talents and be trained professionally. Thus, upon graduating from Lincoln Senior high, he was accepted to attend Julliard School of Music. Here he would welcome his hometown friend, Miles Davis, when his was later accepted. The two had played together in the Lincoln High School band. As a classical pianist, Haynes made his debut at Carnegie Hall in 1958. His performance would prove so electrifying that he would be asked to perform later that same year at the World's Fair in Brussels, Belgium.[57]

His artistry was praised not only in the Unites States, but also in Europe and South America. The esteemed Isador Philipp called him, "One of the greatest musical talents America has produced." His career in music was multifaceted, including work as a composer, a radio host, and a professor. Though his specialty was classical music, he was at home composing gospel and playing jazz. Upon his retirement, he returned to live in his hometown of East St Louis. One of his last performances was in 2005 at Antioch Baptist Church in Saint Louis, MO.[58] This great musical talent departed this life in 2007.

Eugene Haynes Jr. – Julliard Graduate, Classical Pianist, and Legendary East St. Louisan.

John Hicks

Influential Reporter and Diplomat

John Hicks grew up in the South End of East St. Louis during the Great Depression. As an adult, he would reminisce with friends about his experience playing in the Lincoln High School band with jazz legend, Miles Davis. No stranger to hard work and determination, he would enroll at the University of Illinois in the pre-journalism program. In an article in the St. Louis Post-Dispatch, he is said to have been teased by a friend, "What are you going to do with a journalism degree? Work at the Post-Dispatch?"[59] At this time, in the 1940's, there were very few African American reporters at Caucasian newspapers. This is also the reason why many African American newspapers were founded –to report the news from the perspective of an African American reporter to the African American audience.

Upon graduation, Hicks was referred to the St. Louis Post-Dispatch for an interview and was hired by the paper in 1949. He was the first African American journalist hired to work for the newspaper. He would cover and interview arguably the two most influential figures of the Civil Rights Movement – Martin Luther King and Malcolm X. Moreover, because of his interest in international affairs, he would also interview important international figures visiting the St. Louis area. His stint at the newspaper would last 12 years.

In 1950, he took leave the newspaper for a military assignment in Germany. While there, he became fluent in German. Though he would return to the paper, his experience in Germany, along with his knowledge of foreign affairs, would lead to another great career. In 1961, he was called upon to become a foreign service officer with the U.S. Information Agency. He would go on to become a Diplomat for the United States. He held State Department posts in Berlin, Liberia, Greece and Washington. After this, he was named cultural attaché to the U.S. Embassy in South Africa.

In a St. Louis Post-Dispatch article, he is described by his son, Geoff Hicks, as an easy going and unpretentious man. He never bragged, and had only recently mentioned to his adult son about dining with President Nixon (prior to him becoming President); and dining with the then U.S. Attorney General, Robert Kennedy. While dining with Hicks, Kennedy had asked for his advice on an entrée to order that would give him a 'real' German food experience.

A determined young man from the segregated section of East St. Louis, during the most devastating financial times in history, John Hicks transcended his town, his state, and his country to have his voice and opinions heard and respected by the most influential figures in the world.

John Hicks– Reporter, Diplomat, and a Legendary East St. Louisan.

Cecile Hoover-Edwards

Scholar, Researcher, Legendary East St. Louisan

At the very young age of 15, Cecile Hoover graduated from Lincoln High School and set-off to begin her education at the Tuskegee Institute (now Tuskegee University). She quickly completed her studies. By the age of 21, she had already earned her Master's in Chemistry.[60] In 1950, she received her Ph.D. in Nutrition (Food Chemistry) from Iowa State college (now university). That same year[61], she became an Assistant Professor at the Tuskegee Institute. She was just 24 years of age. While at Tuskegee, she worked as a Research Associate at the George Washington Carver Foundation.

She excelled in teaching and research while at Tuskegee; and by 1952 she was the head of the department of Nutrition. She would serve in this position until 1956, when she left to pursue a position at North Carolina A&T State University.

In 1971, she joined the faculty at Howard University. While at Howard she would establish a Doctorial Nutrition Program, the first of its nature at an African American school. She was Dean of the School of Human Ecology from 1974 to 1986, the Dean of the University's School of Continuing Education (1986-87) and Interim Dean of the College of Pharmacy, and Nursing and Allied Health Sciences (1997-98). She continued researching throughout her career.

The focus of her research was on how to make the best foods (healthiest food) for the least amount of money. In the beginning, her research was focused on improving the diets of lower income households. However, as her career and research evolved, she began to focus more on the diet of the African American community, and later on pregnant African American women specifically. Her research focused on a higher protein/lower fat diet. She focused on the amino acid, methionine, and believed that a better diet could improve the health of the mother and the child.

Her research was funded by the National Institute of Food and Agriculture (an agency within the United States Department of Agriculture), the National Science Foundation and the Atomic Energy Commission. As a prolific researcher and writer, she contributed more than 150 articles to scholarly journals in the fields of science and nutrition. At one time serving, as the editor of the Journal of Nutrition –only preeminent scholars are allowed to serve as editors of an educational journal.

In 1991, she published: *Human Ecology: Interactions of Man with His Environments; An Introduction to the Academic Discipline of Human Ecology*. Human Ecology is the study of humans across several different disciplinary fields – nutrition, anthropology, and psychology, to name a few. At that time, she began to look beyond nutrition and focus her studies on ways to improve the overall health and well-being of African-Americans and other minorities. Therefore, she was well-equipped to combat a controversial study published in 1992 by Arthur Jensen. In his work, he stated that the lower scores on IQ tests by African-Americans were the result of genetics. Dr. Edwards challenged this position and concluded that nutrition, psychology, medical care, educational quality and social and environmental factors were contributing factors to the lower scores. [62]

Because of her influential career in the field of nutrition, she was world-renowned expert in the field. She was called as an expert to testify before Congress. She was on several committees for the National Institute of Health and the United States Department of Agriculture. She was also honored by the National Council of Negro Women. In 1984, the State of Illinois declared April 5th to be "Dr. Cecile Hoover-Edwards Day."

Dr. Cecile Hoover-Edwards, Scholar, Researcher, and Legendary East St. Louisan.

Reginald Hudlin

I always carry the Metro-East with me, whatever I'm doing, wherever I go."

Reginald Hudlin was born in East Saint Louis, Illinois on December 15, 1961. Mr. Hudlin is an iconic writer, director, producer, and executive in the entertainment industry. In 2016, he is directing and co-producing the movie *Marshall,* about iconic supreme court justice, Thurgood Marshall. He was a co-producer for the 2016, *88th Academy Award Ceremony*. He produced *Django Unchained*, which in 2012 won The American Film Institute Award for Movie of the Year, Two Golden Globe Awards and was nominated for an Oscar for Best Motion Picture of the Year.

He is a pioneer of African American films and made his debut by writing and directing the movie *House Party* which was said to be based on the house parties that he and his brothers held at their home on Virginia Place in East St. Louis. *House Party*, originally a senior thesis, for his studies at Harvard University would be the impetus to a great career.[63] The success of *House Party* led to his involvement in many of the classic Black films of the 90's. He wrote and produced *BeBe's Kids*. He directed *Boomerang*, *The Great White Hype*, and *The Ladies Man*.

He was the first President of Entertainment for BET, and was responsible for the creation of the BET HIP HOP AWARDs and BET HONORS. Moreover, he was a producer and director on the well received and popular *Bernie Mac Show*. He has served as director on episodes of many popular sitcoms including *Bones, The Office, and Modern Family*.

His talents and interests are varied. He has created graphic novels, Sci-Fi programs, award shows and movies; while also producing, directing, and/or writing some of the most iconic works. On the website, http://hudlinentertainment.com/, readers are able to get a glimpse into his life with information on things that he likes including books, films and music.

Reginald Hudlin is an Iconic Filmmaker and Legendary East St. Louisan.

Warrington Hudlin

Trailblazer in Film

Warrington Hudlin is a native East St. Louisan whose family was instrumental in strengthening the East St. Louis African American community. His father owned a prominent Insurance company in the city. Moreover, due to the family's contributions to the area, they were one of the subjects of a Saint Louis University Archives Exhibit, "Black Elites: Successful People of Color in St. Louis."[64]

He and his brother Reginald Hudlin followed in his great-grandfather, Richard Hudlin's footsteps. "Mr. Richard Hudlin was a journalist, actor, and the third African-American in history to establish a motion picture company."[65] As a journalist, Richard

Hudlin interviewed prominent African-Americans who visited St. Louis and East St. Louis such as W.E.B. Dubois, a national civil rights activist who worked with East St. Louisans to form the local chapter of the NAACP; and Booker T. Washington, founder of the Tuskegee Institute.

After attending Yale University, Warrington Hudlin created the 1978 documentary, *"Black at Yale."*[66] This would prove to be the start of an illustrious career in film. Later, he and his brother Reginald Hudlin would become pioneers of the 90's African American film movement, creating classics such as *House Party, Boomerang* and *Bebe Kids.*

Since that time, Mr. Warrington Hudlin has continued a successful career in both TV and web programming. He produced *Iron Ring* for BET, which was a highly successful reality show on Mixed Martial Arts. The show was one of the highest-rated shows on the network.[67] Moreover, he produced *Cosmic Slop* for HBO, an award-winning trilogy which used the Sci-Fi genre as the framework for thought-provoking content on race relations.

As a member of the film community devoted to public service, he served as the executive producer of BFF lab, a non-profit devoted to the production of works by young minority filmmakers. His work with BFF resulted in a 2005 Webby Award. He continues to blaze trails in Hollywood and continues to promote minority filmmakers through his website dvrepublic.org.

Warrington Hudlin is a Legendary East St. Louisan and a trailblazer in film.

Sam Jethroe

Sam "The Jet" Jethroe 'Could Outrun the Word of God'

Sam Jethroe was nicknamed the Jet because he could run so fast that one of his teammates declared that he could "outrun the word of God." At Lincoln Senior High, he played football, basketball, baseball, and even boxed. His favorite game though was baseball. After graduation, he played for the East Saint Louis Giants, then the East Saint Louis Colts. The Colts were a semi-pro team from which many people were drafted into the Major Leagues.

As a Negro League player, he proved that he was unstoppable. One opponent noticed that Jethroe had a tell; when he was going to steal bases, he would pull up his pants leg. Even with this knowledge, the opponent could not stop him because he was just

74

that fast. The baseball great even beat Olympic Gold Medalist sprinter, Barney Ewell, in a pregame exhibition foot race. But to be a great baseball player you needed more than speed. In 1944 and 1945, the switch-hitter led the league in both batting, and stolen bases with batting averages at .353 and .393 and stolen bases with 18 and 21, respectively. While in the league, Jethroe led his team, The Cleveland Buckeyes, to the Negro American League Pennant with a 4-0 sweep of the Homestead Grays.

Years before Jackie Robinson would become the first African-American in the Major Leagues, Jethroe; Robinson; and Marvin Williams all tried out for the Boston Red Sox, but neither were chosen for the team, despite their prowess as players.

In 1950, Jethroe was the first African-American signed to the Boston Braves, and the sixth African-American in the League. That year, he put his jets on once again and led the league in stolen bases (35) and a batting average of .273. He claimed Rookie of the Year Honors; and to this day, he still remains the record holder for the oldest Rookie of the Year in the League.[68]

Sam "The Jet" Jethroe is a Legendary East Saint Louisan.

Judge Billy Jones

Photo Credit: Ebony Tree

A lawyer, a civil rights advocate, a humanitarian and a Legendary East St. Louisan

An outstanding lawyer and admirable humanitarian, Judge Billy Jones never saw an injustice that he did not want to fight. A standout student at Tennessee State College, Jones would go on to attend law school at Howard University.[69] There, he was also exceptional. He became a member of the Court of Peers and later Chief Justice of Court of Peers. This was a moot court program at Howard University– becoming a member was one of the highest honors that a Howard Law School student could achieve. It is akin to the Huver I. Brown Trial Advocacy Moot Court Team currently at Howard University.[70] In 1945, he graduated from Howard

University School of Law, and quickly began his advocacy for African-Americans.

In 1949, he gained national publicity for attempting to enroll African American children into nine all-white public schools.[71] An avid member of the NAACP, he would later file suit, on behalf of the NAACP, to integrate East St. Louis schools. [72] He was successful in this case, and because of his dogged determination, schools in East St. Louis were integrated. He would also prove successful in integrating schools in Sparta, Illinois and Cairo, Illinois; in 1950 and 1951 respectfully.

Because of his success in the integration of schools in Southern Illinois, he was asked to serve as a consultant and advisor on the historical *Brown v. Board of Education*, which resulted in the Supreme Court's ruling that separate educational facilities were inherently unequal. This decision would be the impetus to the integration of all schools in the United States.

Although he had a great legal mind, and had consulted on one of the largest cases in history, he continued to serve the East St. Louis community; and oftentimes, this service was pro-bono. Moreover, his service went beyond legal service to the community. He was a lifetime member of the NAACP and served as President of the NAACP of Illinois. He served as the Mid-Western Vice-President of his fraternity, Alpha Phi Alpha; National President of the National Bar Association; President of Howard University Law School Alumni Association; and Chairman for the War on Poverty Program for St. Clair County.

Because of his advocacy and distinguished legal career, he was appointed the First Black Associate Judge in the Twelfth Judicial Circuit Court of Illinois; and in 1992, he was inducted posthumously into the National Bar Association Hall of Fame. East St. Louis renamed Monroe Elementary at 1601 Cleveland Ave in his honor.

Judge Billy Jones: a lawyer, a civil rights advocate, a humanitarian and a Legendary East St. Louisan.

Jackie Joyner-Kersee

Photo Credit: Memories4U, Ricky Slaughter

Nationally Defined as One of the Greatest Athletes in History

Native East St. Louisan, Jackie Joyner-Kersee's name is synonymous with greatness. Nationally defined as one of the greatest athletes in history, she is the most decorated female athlete in Olympic track and field history. She and her brother, Olympic Gold Medalist, Al Joyner, would take the world by storm. Her accomplishments in track and field are almost too numerous to name. According to the United States Track and Field website:

> "Jackie Joyner-Kersee's achievements include three Olympic gold medals, four World Outdoor Championship gold medals, and the still-standing world record of 7,291

points in the women's heptathlon. JJK was a four-time Olympian, who won the long jump gold medal in 1988, and long jump bronze in 1992 and 1996. In Olympic heptathlon competition she won the silver medal in 1984 and the gold medal in 1988 and 1992. A four-time World Outdoor Championships team member, she won long jump gold medals in 1987 and 1991, and heptathlon gold in 1987 and 1993. The USA 100m hurdles champion in 1994, JJK won the national long jump title nine times, and the national championship in the heptathlon on eight occasions. During her career at the USA Indoor Championships, she won the 60m hurdles title in 1992, and the long jump national crown in 1992, '94, '95. As a collegian at UCLA, Joyner-Kersee won the NCAA heptathlon title in 1982, 1983. The former long jump world record holder, she set the heptathlon world record three times and was a two-time 100mH U.S. record holder, four-time U.S. long jump record holder, two-time U.S. 60m hurdles record holder and six-time and current U.S. indoor long jump record holder. She is the current U.S. indoor 50mH, 55mH and 60mH record holder. JJK, the first woman ever to break 7,000 points in the heptathlon, was world ranked three times at 100m hurdles, 11 times at LJ (#1 three times) and 11 times in the heptathlon (#1 six times)."[73]

Kersee's greatness was recognized at a young age. Her ambition started with running relays around the block and practicing the long jump off her porch.[74] At the age of nine, she

began running track for the Mary Brown Center located on the

southeast corner of Lincoln Park.   Locals would often encourage

her and revel in her speed and athleticism. She was a stand-out

athlete in track-and-field, basketball and volleyball. She attended

high school at Lincoln Sr. High and trained under Legendary

Coach Nino Fennoy. As a junior in high school, she set an Illinois'

state record in long jump. She would go on to the University of

California, Los Angeles (UCLA).[75] While there, she began to train

for the heptathlon. Before graduating from UCLA, she had already

earned a silver medal in the 1984 Summer Olympics.

After her graduation from UCLA, she would continue her

reign as an Olympic star and World Champion. Her career would

last for many years before her retirement after the 1996 Olympics.

She is the recipient of numerous accolades: a two-time winner of

Jesse Owens Award, noted by Sports Illustrated as the greatest

female athlete of the 20th century, and a USA Track and Field Hall

of Famer.

Her humanitarianism can be noted throughout the country.

She has donated to and helped several organizations through

monetary efforts and time commitment. In 2015, she received a

Lifetime Achievement Award from the National Recreation

Foundation in Rhode Island. Throughout her success, she has

continued to show her devotion to her hometown. She built the

Jackie Joyner-Kersee Center which offers programs in dance,

sports, and early education. She is more than a figurehead for the center. She actively recruits for and participates in events at the center, which serves underprivileged minorities.

Jackie Joyner-Kersee an Olympic Star, a World Champion, a Legendary East St. Louisan, and a local hero.

John Milton Kirkpatrick

A Crusader

John Milton Kirkpatrick, though not a native of East St. Louis was reared in the town. After attending Lincoln University, he would work as a reporter for two African American Publications, the *Saint Louis Call* and the *Argus*. In 1941, he founded the East St. Louis African American newspaper, the *Crusader*.[76] He was also a writer for the publication. In his weekly column, entitled, "As I See It," he focused on the problems and achievements of local African-Americans. The paper was well respected by all because of its adherence to ethics and public service.[77] Because of his contributions, he met with President Lyndon B. Johnson, as one of the select few of the National Newspaper Association who met with the President.[78]

In 1961, Kirkpatrick was appointed as the first director of the Human Rights Commission in East St. Louis.[79] Though an honor, as a result of his involvement with and his appointment to the Human Rights Commission, John Kirkpatrick endured personal and financial setbacks. When he moved his residence to the Lake Drive area, a predominantly white neighborhood, his home was burned. Undeterred, he continued in the civil rights struggle. As an investigator for the State's Attorney's Office, he vigorously pursued his responsibility to safeguard the civil rights of East St. Louis citizens.[80] In 1967, a firebomb was thrown into the offices of the *Crusader Newspaper*.[81] Luckily, there was little damage to the building and no one was hurt. The perpetrators were never found.

The *Crusader* served the community of East St. Louis for almost 23 years, save for the three years that Kirkpatrick served in the Army. It was known for its Annual Crusader Kids Picnic and Annual Mother of the Year Award.

In 1972, when Kirkpatrick died, James Williams (the first African American mayor of East St. Louis) said of Kirkpatrick, "East St. Louis has suffered an almost irreparable loss…he was a man well esteemed by both Black and White, young and old, rich and poor, learned and unlearned. He was a leader of a very high caliber, a Christian gentleman and a worthy civil rights advocate for the people."[82]

John Kirkpatrick– a Legendary East St. Louisan.

Mrs. Mary Martin

Photo Credit: Ebony Tree

She was a fervent friend and advocate for her fellow women, a mother to needy children, and a companion for the elderly.

During the early 1900's, there was very little aid for impoverished citizens or communities. It was not uncommon to see minority children who had been essentially abandoned and left to fend for themselves on the streets. Many resorted to petty crimes just to survive. Mrs. Mary Martin led the charge to assure that these children had someone on their side. In 1910[83], Mrs. Martin and her fellow female East St. Louisan started what would later become the Colored Old Folks' Home and Orphans' Association.

The organization was chartered in 1913 with Mrs. Mary Martin as President; Mrs. Mary Parris as Vice- President; Mrs. Albert McKenzie as Secretary; and Mrs. Moore as Treasurer. According to *Discovering African American St. Louis*, Mrs. Martin started the organization by caring for homeless and orphaned children in her home. When the number became too many to serve in her home, she moved the operation to a basement in Friendship Baptist Church. The Colored Old Folks' Home and Orphans' Association helped in 1917, after what has been called a 'Massacre' or 'Pogrom' (a violent riot aimed at an ethnic group), the East St. Louis Race Riots. Many families were not only physically violated (burned, killed and shot), but were financially violated – having their homes looted for valuables and burned to ashes. Many returned to their homes with nothing and the organization that she founded was there to provide them with food, clothing and other items.

In 1918, she would go on to become one of the first members of the East St. Louis Chapter of the Urban League which began in that same year. The Urban League of St. Louis was founded as a result of the 1917 East St. Louis Riots. Martin was later a member of the prominent Colored Women's Republican Club, a bipartisan organization that educated woman on the political arena – how to organize and seek party nominations. The organization actively supported women's political campaigns. They were successful in getting Eliza Hart (Democrat) and Nevada Hamilton (Republican)

elected in 1928. They were the first two African American
Precinct Committee (wo)men in East St. Louis.

Moreover, Mrs. Martin was a member of the Colored
Women's Welfare League. In the 1930's, with the help of
Elizabeth Nash and other members of the organization, the league
formed a 'Better Babies' program which addressed the deplorable
conditions of health in the African American community. Many
were not receiving adequate healthcare –due to hospital
segregation. African-Americans were rarely treated well or seen in
the hospitals in East St. Louis. They had to travel to St. Louis for
basic care.

In 1937, with the help of the members and 'boosters'– Mrs.
Sarah Flood, Mrs. Racheal Ingram, Mrs. Ruth Freeman and Mrs.
Annie McCraven, who raised funds– the organization moved to its
new place: The Mary Martin Center at 1945 Market Street.
Through the Mary Martin Center, The Colored Old Folks' Home
and Orphans' Association, began to provide healthcare services
and education. The center would go on to serve the community,
which it helped strengthen for almost 50 years. For some years, it
would also serve as a place for social gatherings for civic
organizations and private citizens.

Mrs. Mary Martin was a pillar of the East St. Louis
community. She was a fervent friend and advocate for her fellow
women, a mother to needy children, and a companion for the
elderly. Mrs. Mary Martin –a Legendary East St. Louisan.

Brother Joe May

The Greatest Male Gospel Singer in History

Though born in Macon, Mississippi, Brother Joe May chose East St. Louis as the place to raise his family. He began singing while still in Macon, Mississippi, at the tender age of nine. Before moving north, he had established himself in the Southern gospel circles – singing with the Little Church Out on the Hills Senior Choir.[84]

Upon moving north, he began working at the Monsanto Chemical plant.[85] However, he would continue singing. Here, he would be mentored by Willie May Ford Smith – considered to be one of the most legendary gospel singers. Under the tutelage of his mentor, he sang in multiple Thomas A. Dorsey's National Convention of Gospel Choirs and Choruses. Through these events, he became known nationwide. A tenor, May's voice was said to easily transition from just above a whisper to shaking the rafters of the Church –leading to his stage name given by Smith, "The Thunderbolt of the Midwest."

In 1949, he was signed to Specialty Records and would release, "Search Me Lord" and "Do You Know Him," in 1950. Both albums were well received by audiences; and due to their popularity, May became a household name, often being compared to Mahalia Jackson. He sometimes performed with the famed gospel singer and was called the Male Mahalia Jackson, as his voice was as powerful and controlled as hers. However, he would not crossover as she did to Caucasian audiences. Nevertheless, he would prove successful enough in the African American community to sustain his family on his career singing. Later in his career, he would move on to the label Nashboro, and release other singles such as "Don't Let the Devil Ride." He would also star in the musical *Black Nativity* which enjoyed much success throughout the country and in Europe. Throughout his success, the May family continued to call East St. Louis home.

Brother Joe May, a Legendary East St. Louisan is considered to be the greatest male gospel singer in history.

U.S. Ambassador Donald McHenry

Photo Credit: I Am EStL, The Magazine/ Stephen Bennett

Advisor to World Leaders

Donald McHenry is a native of East St. Louis; however, he was born in 1936 in St. Louis, MO, due to segregationist policies in East St. Louis Hospitals. In 1957, he would graduate from Illinois State University. As a student at the University, he was a founding member of a local chapter of the NAACP.[86] He would go on to receive his Master's in Political Science from Southern Illinois University at Carbondale.[87] After graduating, he began lecturing at Howard University and pursuing further studies at Georgetown.

In 1963, before the age of 30, McHenry would begin to make his mark at the State Department. In 1966, he would receive the Department of State's Superior Honor Award for his achievements within the department.[88] He served the State Department in various capacities until 1971. In 1971, due to President Nixon's policies on the Vietnam War, he chose to take a leave of absence.[89] While on leave, he was Guest Scholar at the Brookings Institution and an International Affairs Fellow at the Council on Foreign Relations.[90] He had hoped that Nixon would lose the 1973 election, so that he could return to the department; however, that was not the case; therefore, he made the choice to resign from the department.

However, in the late 70's he was able to return to the State Department. He worked on President Carter's State Department Transition Team. He served as Ambassador and U.S. Permanent Representative to the United Nations (U.N.). While in this position, he served as the U.S. Deputy Representative to the United Nations Security Council, and served as a delegate to the U.N. International Conference on Human Rights. Later, he was the chief negotiator on Namibia's Independence from the South African Apartheid System, a member of the United Nations Panel on Algeria, and a consultant to President Bill Clinton on Nigeria.

As the founder of the IRC Group, an international consulting firm, McHenry has advised and served on the boards of several multinational companies including: The Coca-Cola Company, Fleet Boston Financial, AT&T, GlaxoSmithKline and many others. In 2014, when he retired from the board of the Coca-Cola

Company, Muhtar Kent, the CEO said of McHenry, "In addition to his stellar career as a diplomat and respected public servant, he has spent countless hours working for our Board and on behalf of our Company – for which we are honored. Notably, in 1985, Don signed on as the inaugural chair of our Public Issues and Diversity Review Committee and he led this important work until 2012. He has been a great advisor to me and we have all gained from his clear direction and leadership."[91]

Moreover, he has also excelled in academia. Upon his retirement from Georgetown as a Distinguished Professor in the Practice of Diplomacy at the School of Foreign Service, the University established the Donald F. McHenry Chair in Global Human Development.

Even in retirement, McHenry is a highly sought after advisor. Ambassador Donald McHenry is a Legendary East St. Louisan.

Claudia Nash- Thomas

A Torchbearer, Leading the Way for Her Community

Mrs. Claudia Nash-Thomas was a trailblazer. A native of East Saint Louis, her community involvement served to nurture and build the African-American community in East St. Louis. After graduating from Southern Illinois University at Carbondale, she became a teacher in Sparta, IL; but her commitment to her community would bring her home to serve the very school district that helped to mold her into the leader that she became.

Mrs. Nash-Thomas was on the forefront of the Civil Rights Movement. Seeing the need for equality in East St. Louis, Mrs. Nash-Thomas joined the East St. Louis branch of the NAACP. Her involvement quickly evolved from member to secretary to president of the organization. In 1946, Mrs. Nash-Thomas took the helm of the East St. Louis Branch of the NAACP. Under her leadership, the organization flourished. With the assistance of W.K. Allen, Spencer Jackson, David Owens and the Perry brothers,[92] a successful membership drive garnered 500 new members to the organization. As president, her commitment to the education of the city's youth continued. She established a tutoring program headed by Alice Lucas and Clementine Reeves-Harris. Moreover, she began laying the groundwork for the integration of public schools in the city, which was later spearheaded by a local businessman, Robert Perry Storman, and NAACP members – Attorney Billy Jones and David Owens (president in 1949). Under her leadership, the organization also sponsored a Well-Baby Clinic under the direction of Nurse Goldie Hill and Dr. John Eubanks, a well-respected African American doctor and East St. Louis citizen as well.

Not only was she a valuable leader and member of the N.A.A.C. P., but she was committed to a number of other community-based organizations including The Mental Health Association, Emily Willis Day Care Center, St. Luke A.M.E. Church, Community Concert, United Way, Children's Center for Behavioral Development, and the Y.W.C. A.

Her tireless service resulted in numerous awards. She was the United Way Woman of the Year in 1977. She received the Y.M.C.A.'s President's Service Award in 1982, the Profile of

Prominence Award in 1982 from the Metro-East Woman of Achievement, and a twenty-five-year service award from the United Way. In August 1980, due to her accomplishments and esteemed reputation, she was called on by then Governor James R. Thompson to serve her community further. He appointed her to the East St. Louis Financial Advisory Authority.

Mrs. Claudia Nash-Thomas, a torchbearer, and a Legendary East St. Louisan.

Fredericka Nash and M Frances Nash Terrell

Fredericka

The Nash Family is the owner of Nash Funeral Home, the area's oldest African American funeral home.[93]

Before Claudia, Fredericka, and Frances were born, Nash Funeral Home and Cremation Service would open its doors in 1913 as The Nash Brothers Undertaking Company. The girls' father, Charles Nash, also referred to as C.T. Nash, and his brothers owned the business. However, the business would suffer a great setback in 1917, when it was burned during the 1917 Race Riots.[94] Mr. Charles Nash is credited with saving lives during the riots by transporting African-Americans to St. Louis in a company hearse. After the riots, the business would be reestablished by Charles Nash as C.T. Nash Funeral Home. C.T. Nash and his wife, would have three lovely daughters: Claudia, Fredericka and Frances. He would groom his daughters to take over his businesses, and each did share in her responsibility to the business and to the city.

As an adult, Frances Nash-Terrell would stand as CEO of Nash Funeral Home until her death in 2003. Her service to the community went beyond that though. Mrs. Nash-Terrell was a lifetime member of the NAACP, and when she found that there was a lack of minorities involved in the construction of the Orr-Weathers Homes, she worked with other members, Judge Billy Jones and David Owens to launch a successful campaign to have more African-Americans hired for the project.[95]

Moreover, due to budgetary constraints, many of the police officers and firefighters of the city were helping citizens at the risk of their own safety. Therefore, she founded the East St. Louis Volunteers for Police and Fire Safety, an organization launched to raise funds for safety equipment needed by the departments. Some of the funds raised went to walkie-talkies for police and bulletproof vests. Moreover, she established the NAACP Scholarship fund; and she donated her time to many civic organizations.

Although all of the sisters worked in the business, Fredericka Nash would take the reins of the business after her sister's death. As a lifetime member of the NAACP, the family would offer free space to the organizations for meetings. She was described by former mayor, Alvin Parks, in a Belleville News-Democrat article about her death as "a courageous, stalwart business person."[96] She was the first African American woman to serve on the school board, and a woman of many talents –lecturer, trainer, and writer.

The Nash Family members are Legendary East St. Louisans.

Marion E. Officer Sr.

Photo Credit: officerfh.com

Marion E. Officer Sr., a Man for all Seasons, Son of a Legend

Officer Funeral Home was established by William and Annette Officer in 1918, officially opening on December 16, 1918.[97] At that time, they moved the funeral home into a previously constructed building at 2101 Missouri Ave. It was a two-story building with apartments and a store. In 1929, looking to better serve the African American community, the family built one of the first funeral homes in Southern Illinois designed specifically as a funeral home. [98]

Marion E. Officer Sr., son of William and Annette Officer and a native of East St. Louis graduated from Lincoln Sr. High in 1940.

From there he would further his education at Morehouse College and Howard University to name a few of the places he attended to further his education. He was inducted into the Army in 1943 and fought in World War II. Some years after returning home, he would graduate from the St. Louis College of Mortuary Science in 1952. In 1954, Marion Officer Sr. and his wife, Myrtle Officer took the helm of the family business.

He was known as a respectable and generous businessman. He donated to churches, giving: stained glass windows, pianos, organs, and other things as needed. He offered funeral services to families pro-bono when they could not afford services. He was a prominent member of the NAACP and gave space to the NAACP for group meetings for over twenty years. "Because of his long-standing consistent support and contributions, Mr. Officer was bestowed the Humanitarian Award in 1987 by the local branch."[99] He personally paid to send children of the city to college, and because of this, a scholarship was developed in his name.

He served on the board of directors for Union National Bank in East St. Louis, the first African-American to do so. He was on the executive board of the NAACP and St. Mary's Hospital in East St. Louis. He was a member of several organizations, including The Gold Star Church Aid Society, the Urban League and the Business and Professional Men's Club of East St. Louis, plus many more.[100]

Before his death, he was able to see his son, the young, 27-year-old Carl E. Officer elected mayor. Marion E. Officer Sr., a man for all seasons, son of a legend and a Legendary East St. Louisan.

Dr. Lillian Parks

Photo Credit: I Am EStL, The Magazine/ Stephen Bennett

Dr. Lillian Adams Parks, Daughter of Legends, Mother to Legends

The daughter of an East St Louis pioneer, Horace Adams, Dr. Lillian Parks became a leader herself, and is the mother to two leaders, former Mayor Alvin Parks and Lauren Parks-Goins.

Dr. Parks completed her B.A. at the University of Illinois, her M.A. at Washington University and her doctorate at Saint Louis University. Though the daughter of a prominent East St. Louisan, Dr. Parks reached her position through hard work and determination. After completing her education, she returned in 1954 to teach English at her alma mater, Lincoln High School. As an English teacher she would work on Project Speak a program written and directed by her sister, Vivian Adams. Project Speak was an all-language program for disadvantaged students. As an English teacher, she was described by many as excellent.

She worked in several capacities within the school district before being asked to serve as Interim Superintendent of District 189 in 1989. While assigned to her new post, board member Ed Jucewicz was quoted in a St. Louis Post-Dispatch article as saying, "She has established a very good climate of trust, cooperation and unity. She was excellent. She pays attention to details, and she operates with complete openness with no hidden agenda or back room politics."[101] Parks was a breath of fresh air to a district that had been plagued by rumors and innuendo of misappropriated funds and secrecy. Due to her compelling work while serving as Interim Superintendent, she was appointed as the first woman Superintendent of the East St. Louis School District 189. At the time she was Superintendent, she said of the students, "Gifted children are everywhere in East St. Louis, but their gifts are lost to poverty and turmoil and the damage done by knowing they are written off by society."[102]

Parks' goal seemed to be to assure these children that they were not alone in society. She fought diligently for the youth of East St. Louis, and served on several boards within the community to help strengthen the community. She served on the Board of St. Mary's Hospital, The Urban League, Junior Achievement, and the Katherine Dunham Center to name a few. She personally sold engraved bricks to help fund the Jackie Joyner-Kersee Youth

Center. She sent letters to schools, churches, organizations, and volunteer groups for support.

Moreover, Dr. Parks has contributed to preserving the history of East St. Louis. She has been acknowledged by Andrew Theising in his work *Made in USA: East St. Louis The Rise and Fall of an Industrial River Town* and in *American Pogrom: The East St. Louis Race Riots and Black Politics*. Furthermore, she, with several members of Delta Sigma Theta Sorority, was instrumental in publishing the manuscript *The Ebony Tree* by Mrs. Clementine Reeves-Hamilton. *The Ebony Tree* served to preserve the history of African-Americans in East St. Louis and has been referenced by several works on East St. Louis.

One article is not enough to cover the career of Dr. Lillian Parks who retired in 1993 after over 50 years in district 189 serving in one capacity or another as either a student, teacher or administrator. [103] For her years of service, she has received innumerable awards. She was awarded the Lifetime Achievement award by both the St. Louis Community Empowerment Foundation and the NAACP. She was listed as one of the 100 Most Influential Blacks. She was given The Woman of the Year award by the East St. Louis *Monitor*, the Outstanding Citizen Award by the *St. Louis Argus*, and the Sammy Davis Jr. "Yes I Can" award for outstanding educational leadership.[104]

Dr. Lillian Adams Parks, daughter of legends, mother to legends, and a Legendary East St. Louisan.

Edna Patterson-Petty

To me, art is being able to take things that others throw away or discard and turn it into some things of beauty.

Her quilts tell a story that weaves through the fabric of experiences of all mankind. Her artistry speaks of our history, our triumphs and our weaknesses. For this reason, Edna Patterson-Petty's work is extolled not only in her hometown or even America, but by people in foreign lands, such as Beijing, China; Senegal, Africa; Ottawa, Canada; and Islamabad, Pakistan, who identify with her work which exemplifies 'the human condition.' Whether it is her latest quilt, created to educate on the deadly 1917 Riots of East St. Louis, which symbolizes the cruelties of mankind; or her quilt, "If it Wasn't for the Women," which was constructed to represent the strength of all women, there is a visceral connection to her art that supersedes religious, ethnic and racial boundaries. Her works speak a universal language that isn't muddied by words. She says of her gift, "I know that my creative ability is of divine inspiration, because I dream art, I feel art, I get excited when I am around art, and through my creations I reveal my internal world."

Though she is known for her quilts, one of which, "Road to Redemption," was exhibited in Washington D.C. for the celebration of President Obama's Inauguration, her artistry extends beyond fabric work. She has works displayed throughout the St. Louis Metropolitan area. She created mosaic tiled benches in Jones Park in East St. Louis. When the Southern Illinois University, East St. Louis (SIU-ESL) campus was built, she was commissioned to create the beautifully sculptured turtles which adorn the campus. "A Whimsical View" can be seen at Lambert-St. Louis International at Gate A8. To create this piece, which she describes as "a deconstructed quilt," Mrs. Patterson-Petty was chosen as one of only nine artists to travel to Munich, Germany, to study with the esteemed Franz Mayer & Co., known internationally for their glass artwork.

She has received many awards, such as The Grand Center Visionary Award, Community Art in Education Award, the NAACP Arts Award, a Community Arts Award, and many more. In 2010, she was honored by her alma mater, Southern Illinois University at Edwardsville with the SIUE Wall of Fame Alumni Award.

A life-long resident of East St. Louis and a graduate of SIUE with an M.F.A. in Textile Art and an M.A. in Art Therapy, Mrs. Patterson-Petty says that she has always wanted to be an artist. She says of art, "To me, art is being able to take things that others throw away or discard and turn it into some things of beauty or some things of interest — just being able to take a mundane situation or a mundane thing and turn it into something viable and just give things life." To fellow East St. Louisans, she would advise, "Know Your History"; and rightly so as it is filled with Legends such as Edna Patterson-Petty, a Legendary East St. Louisan.

Reginald Petty

Curator of East St. Louis Legends and a Legend Himself

Upon reviewing his personal motto, **"In order to know where you are going, you have to know where you come from,"** one can begin to understand why Mr. Reginald Petty has amassed such an extensive collection of East St. Louis History. Going through his files, one can only begin to understand why he is the authority on all things East St. Louis. He has accumulated a treasure trove of information about the city, that is unrivaled even by local libraries. In fact, he rescued historical information about the city from the abandoned library on Martin Luther King Drive. You want information about the 1917 Riots, he has the files. You want information about the founding of the city, the first Mayor, or the first African American Mayor, he has the information. You want to know who were some of the greatest scholars, artists and athletes from the great city of East St. Louis, as the city's unofficial historian, Mr. Petty can recite those to you with no use of notes, and if you need the documentation, he has it.

Mr. Reginald Petty, is a native of East St. Louis, and a current resident; but before he came home, he blazed roads in civil rights, education, and international relations. He took on the banner of social injustices while still in college. While attending Southern Illinois University at Carbondale, he became aware that African-Americans couldn't adopt, his reporting on this issue was forwarded to Congress and led to the changing of legislation. After earning his Master's in Education and Sociology, his urge to play a greater role in the Civil Rights Movement led him to Mississippi, where he became a member of the Student Non-Violent Coordinating Committee (SNCC), an instrumental organization in the Civil Rights Movement. As a SNCC member, he fought against government sanctioned discrimination which sought to disenfranchise African-Americans.

After his work in Mississippi, he was hand-picked to establish information for the first Job Corps in the United States. His input and guidance on the educational program at Job Corp were the blueprint for Job Corps educational practices. He served as Executive Director of the National Advisory Council on Vocational/Technical Education, a 21-member council appointed by President Lyndon B. Johnson, which systematized information on the method each state used to manage their vocational and technical educational programs in the United States. Then, in his career at Peace Corps he would travel across the world. He served as the Director of Peace Corps in Kenya, Burkina Faso, Swaziland and the Seychelles.

Due to his work in Africa, he became a highly sought after consultant to African countries such as Egypt, Ethiopia, and Mali. He helped in establishing administrative systems, educational research, and developing plans for funding of educational, agricultural, and economic development.

Mr. Petty and his wife, esteemed artist Edna Patterson-Petty, currently live in East St. Louis. He says of East St. Louis, "In spite of the difficulties that the city has had to overcome, it continues to be a place from which great people in every field have called home;" and for him, "it always has been, and always will be home."

Mr. Reginald Petty, Civil Rights Activist, Former Director of Peace Corps, Consultant to African Nations, East St. Louis Historiographer, and a Legendary East St. Louisan.

Dr. Lorna Polk

Government Administrator Who Soared to Great Heights

Dr. Lorna Polk was a native East St. Louisan who soared to great heights. After graduating from Fisk University, The George Washington University, and The Catholic University of America; she would decide to leave her city to serve her country. She built a career dedicated to the education of Americans.

In 1987, she served under President Ronald Reagan as an Education Specialist for the White House Initiative on Historically Black Colleges and Universities. She would serve the Department of Education for over 40 years and was a Senior Program Officer. In addition to her career at the U.S. Dept. Of Education, she became a licensed pilot. This was also a successful venture.

Thus, her membership in civic organizations was varied and many. She was a founding member of Blacks in Government, the American Society of Professional and Executive Women; Phi Delta Kappa; Toastmasters, Tuskegee Airmen, Inc., and the Organization of Black Airline Pilots. She would later become a board member of the Organization of Black Airline Pilots.

Because of her achievements in both fields, she was given several awards – U.S. Department of Education Special Service Award, Tuskegee Airman Award of the Year for Achievement, National Honoree for Women in Aviation Awards, Outstanding Young Women of America, Who's Who in America, and Who's Who amongst African-Americans.[105]

Dr. Lorna Polk, a government administrator who soared to great heights and a Legendary East St. Louisan.

Dr. Eugene B. Redmond

Photo Credit: *I Am EStL, The Magazine/* Kevin Hopkins

Scholar, Activist, Poet Laureate of East St. Louis

"The poor people of the United States are venting their frustrations, anguish and hatred in gushes of violence....While some pass the riots off as criminally-inspired and the work of thieves and agitators, a study of history and present urban conditions indicate that a revolution is taking place –especially in the ghettos of American Cities."[106] These words, though reminiscent of recent riots in Ferguson, MO, and Baltimore, MD, were written almost five decades ago by poet, professor, scholar, activist, , playwright and photographer, Dr. Eugene Redmond.

Eugene B. Redmond was raised by his grandmother in East St. Louis, after being placed in her charged by his father following the death of his mother when he was nine years old. He would begin a career in writing and photography while still in junior high school at Hughes Quinn.[107] His love for literature, sparked by one of his Lincoln High School teachers, John Caldwell, would send him to Southern Illinois University East St. Louis, after graduating from Lincoln. His first attempt at completing his Bachelors in Literature would be interrupted by service in the Marine Corp. His love for writing though would not be interrupted as he often wrote poetry for *The Leather Neck*, a marine magazine. While serving in Southeast Asia, Redmond would find the poverty and close-knit cultural life to be similar to his own experiences living in the segregated South End of East St. Louis. Later, he would balk at the hypocrisy of the notion of American Exceptionalism, when African-Americans weren't 'free' enough to share the same hospitals, schools, or neighborhoods with their Caucasian-American counterparts.

He would graduate from SIUE with a degree in English (1964) and from Washington University in St. Louis, with a Master's in English in 1966, [108] and begin a mission in activism through the arts. He would write for several newspapers, and serve as an editor of Clyde C. Jordan's The East St. Louis *Monitor* (which he helped start in 1963 while still an SIU student). The first lines of this biographical synopsis were written in "Monitoring the News" a weekly editorial in the *Monitor* by Dr. Redmond. A close friend to Amiri Baraka, Redmond would become a leader, in the Midwest, of the Black Arts Movement– the artistic branch of the Civil

Rights and Black Power Movements. He, along with other prominent writers at the time, such as Nikki Giovanni, Gwendolyn Brooks and Sonia Sanchez, was prominent in the Movement, counted by Baraka as soldiers in the civil rights fight. They wrote of the 'Black experience' in America and of their Black heroes like Malcolm X. Their work was often categorized as radical and not literature. Redmond's documentation of the movement through pictures, letters, flyers, clippings, etc. housed in the Eugene B Redmond Collection and Learning Center at SIUE has the potential to be the library's "most distinct feature and one of the university's greatest scholarly assets" according to Regina McBride, Dean of Library and Information Services.

He is the author/editor of 25 volumes of poetry, collections of diverse writings, plays for stage and TV, and posthumously published works of Henry Dumas. In 1968, his first pamphlet, *A Tale of Two Toms, or Tom-Tom: Uncle Toms of East St Louis & St. Louis* was published. One of his most notable books, *Drumvoices: The Mission of Afro-American Poetry, A Critical History* is a study of poetry from 1746 to 1976 of famous and little known African American Poets; this influential survey set the standard for the compilation of literary works.[109] He, along with the Eugene B. Redmond Writers Club, is the creator of the poetry form the Kwansaba. The Kwansaba, which relates to the tenets of Kwanzaa, is a praise poem that is seven lines long, with seven words in each line, and no word has more than seven letters.

Created in 1995, the Kwansaba has seen a rapid growth in popularity in the last few years.

His awards are numerous including a National Endowment for the Arts Creative Writing Fellowship (NEA), the Sterling Brown Award from ALA's African American Literature and Culture Association, a Lifetime Achievement Award from Pan-African Movement USA, a Pushcart Prize: Best of the Small Presses, two American Book Award, and Writing Fellowships from the California, Illinois, Louisiana, Missouri, and West Virginia Arts Councils.

Besides his writing, photography and activism, Dr. Redmond is also a well-respected scholar who has been teaching since the 1960's. He has held positions at California State University-Sacramento and served as visiting professor and/or lecturer at universities throughout the United States and overseas. In 2008, he received an Honorary Doctorate of Humane Letters from SIUE. And recently, the Professor Emeritus retired from SIUE. He still, however, is active as a writer, lecturer and activist.

Dr. Eugene B. Redmond is a Poet Laureate of East St. Louis and a Legendary East St. Louisan.

Captain John Robinson

Civil War Vet, Educational leader

In the late 1800's, African-Americans in East St. Louis took on the battle of segregated schools. Many were concerned with the lack of proper educational resources for African American children in the city. As late as 1875, there was only one colored 'school,' which was one classroom in First Baptist Church with one teacher, Mr. Moss, and 27 students.[110] African American parents began protests and valiantly attempted to enroll their children in White schools. The city, however, refused to allow African-Americans into White schools; and though the district had agreed to offer a school for African-Americans, they had, to this point, failed to follow through. One person, a former slave and Civil War Veteran, Captain John Robinson,[111] became the leader in this fight to establish a school for the African American children of East St. Louis.[112]

Though he himself had not attended school and could not write his name,[113] he understood the need for education for the youth of East St Louis. Robinson consistently lobbied the school board and his persistence was rewarded with meager amenities– two classrooms above a blacksmith shop on Collinsville Road. Unhappy with the space provided, Robinson continued his pursuit of a decent school for the youth. He worked with local White politicians offering African American votes in exchange for voting for an African American school. According to the *Ebony Tree*, in 1881 he marched children from their 'school' above the blacksmith shop to Clay school– an all Caucasian school, located in a large two-story building at the Southeast corner of Collinsville and St. Louis Ave. The children took seats at the school next to their Caucasian counterparts. This is what is believed to be the tipping point for the school board.

In 1886, a school was established for African-American children in East St. Louis. It was built in an old frame church at sixth street and St. Louis Avenue. His efforts further led to the building of Lincoln Grade and High school at 11th and Broadway (the school was also called Lincoln Polytechnic High School). Students were taught, electricity, plastering, band, cooking and sewing. In June, there was a yearly picnic held in Jones Park. There were many activities, including the wrapping of the Maypole, a tradition that is continued by Dunbar Elementary School.

Robinson also founded the East St. Louis Afro-American Protective League which sought to fight against prejudices and racial injustices. The group served to empower the African American community and its businesses, and condemned violence against African-Americans. The group was highly successful in bargaining African American votes to the political party who was most willing to serve the interests of African-Americans.

When Robinson died in 1918,[114] his life was celebrated. Local newspapers, Black and White, wrote about his influence in the community. His funeral was held in the auditorium of the school he helped establish, Lincoln Grade and High School. John Robinson School, in district 189, was established in his memory. John Robinson's public housing was also named in his honor.

John Robinson is a Legendary East St. Louisan.

Reverend Johnny Scott

Photo Credit: ESLNAACP.org

He stood and gave voice to a community through 30 years of progress and setbacks, celebration and injury.

Reverend Johnny Scott, as a young boy, moved from his hometown of Indianola, Mississippi to East St. Louis. Scott is an entrepreneur, a veteran, a community leader, pastor and a civil rights leader, who has sought to preserve the rights of and create opportunities for minorities in East St. Louis and the State of Illinois.

Formally educated at Mildred Louis Business College in East St. Louis and later LaSalle University in Chicago, Reverend Scott established Scott's Accounting & Tax Services in the city.[115] He would later complete his Theological studies at Midwest

Theological Seminary. Always an active member of the community, he has served as the president of the East St. Louis Police and Fire Board, and as a member of the East St. Louis Housing Authority Board.

In 1982, Reverend Scott was asked to lead the East St. Louis Chapter of the NAACP. Though apprehensive about the position, he became the longest-serving leader in the history of the chapter. In this position, Reverend Scott has fought racial discrimination in housing, employment, and education – targeting civil rights violations in Belleville, Cahokia, Fairview Heights, O'Fallon, and Washington Park.[116] He brought awareness to racially motivated violence and harassment in the community and in municipal and county governments. To this point, he launched a successful campaign for the resignation of Don W. Weber, Madison County Assistant State's Attorney, and for the demotion from committee assignments of Ed Anderson, a Clay County Board Member, for racist statements.

His extensive civil rights advocacy includes the winning of a court order in 1987 to reopen the Eads Bridge to pedestrian traffic during the Veiled Prophet Fair (VP Fair); successful negotiations to increase minority subcontracts for construction work on the Martin Luther King Bridge in 1988; and the establishment in May 1991 of employment standards for minorities for a projected civilian airport at Scott Air Force Base. Reverend Scott has also spearheaded numerous investigations into over assessed taxes on residential property and into insurance company redlining in East

St. Louis – charging exorbitant premiums for East St. Louis residents. Equally important, he has fought for lower income citizens of East St. Louis by exposing the problems of bond for deeds' practices that leave helpless "home buyers" owing more for their residences than initially contracted for and having little or no recourse in the law against unscrupulous realtors.

Moreover, Reverend Scott's vigilance and perseverance have been evident in his economic challenge for the metro area. He launched Operation Fair Share, a project devised by the national office of the NAACP to promote equality in opportunities for African American businesses, and to assure the availability of higher level positions in business for qualified African-Americans. Moreover, he urged the community to participate in Black Dollar Days to demonstrate the African American community's fiscal strength. He promoted higher education among the youth of East St. Louis by assuring that thousands of students received scholarships.

Because of his long service to the community, Reverend Scott was honored by fellow East St. Louisan, Senator Richard Durban who read his name into the National Congressional Records, and said this in his Capitol Hill Tribute:

> Mr. President, Reverend Johnny Scott has announced his retirement after 31 years as president of the NAACP East St. Louis Chapter. On behalf of a grateful community, I thank the Reverend Scott, his wife Gretta Scott and his

three children. He stood and gave voice to a community through 30 years of progress and setbacks, celebration and injury. His leadership has touched East St. Louis deeply. It has been an honor to work alongside Reverend Scott, and Loretta[117] and I wish him and his family the best as he opens the next chapter in his life.[118]

Reverend Scott is a community activist and Legendary East St. Louisan.

Dr. Barbara Ann Teer

She Built a Theater, a Community, Devoted to The Celebration of
Blackness

She was an actor, a dancer, a producer, a writer, a director, a cultural ambassador, and an iconic visionary who saw beyond her station as a young Black girl born in the segregated, Blacks only, South End section of East St. Louis. Even at a young age, Dr. Barbara Ann Teer showed promise. She graduated high school early and went on to major in Dance at the University of Illinois, where she graduated magna cum laude. She would go on to study Dance in Berlin and Paris, and tour with the revolutionary modern dancer, Martha Graham.[119]

After her studies, she moved to New York to further her career. There, she starred in numerous shows both on Broadway and Off-Broadway. She was dance captain in the Tony Award-nominated, *Kwamina*; and won a Drama Desk Award for her role in *Home Movies*. Her acting earned her many accolades, and despite her great success, she decided to leave 'mainstream theater' due to its lack of diverse roles for African-Americans.

In 1968, Dr. Teer wrote in a *New York Times* article, "We must begin building cultural centers where we can enjoy being free, open and Black. Where we can find out how talented we really are, where we can be what we were born to be and not what we were brainwashed to be, where we can 'blow our minds' with Blackness."[120] That same year, she founded the revolutionary National Black Theatre in Harlem, an institution devoted to the support and promotion of Black Art, Black Artists, and the Black Community. Her theater was an influential institution during the Black Arts Movement, often referred to as the artistic branch of the Civil Right Movement. Those in the Black Arts Movement through artistic expression: poetry, dance, theatre, etc. fought against injustices by celebrating the multifaceted nature of Black Culture and History. Though the Black Arts Movement began in New York, its influence would spread nationwide. Dr. Eugene Redmond, also of East St. Louis, is a noted leader of the Black Arts Movement in the Midwest. The National Black Theatre was a success, touring in Haiti, South Africa, Trinidad, Bermuda, Guyana and throughout the United States.

Dr. Teer sought to uplift not only the image of the African-American, but also the Harlem Community. She succeeded in both. Because of her success, she has been awarded several honorary Doctorate degrees. The National Black Theatre is currently in its 47th season, and thriving under the tutelage of Dr. Teer's daughter Sade Lythcott.[121] If you visit New York try to visit the theater started by a Legendary East St. Louisan, Dr. Barbara Ann Teer. For more on the theater, visit nationalblacktheatre.org.

"Black Art is a healing art, and It has the ability to heal the world."

– Dr. Barbara Ann Teer

Leon Thomas

Musical Innovator, Creator of 'Soularfone.'

Before performing with some of the greatest artists of the 60's, 70's, 80's and 90's, Leon Thomas was just a young boy in East St. Louis who had dreams of becoming a singer. Thomas, a native of East St. Louis was born in 1937. By the time he graduated from East St. Louis High School, he had already made inroads towards fulfilling his dreams. He was singing in local choirs and performing with acts such as Jimmy Forrest[122] and Grant Green.[123]

After graduating from high school, he would go to Tennessee State University (TSU) to study music. In 1958, two years after leaving TSU, he would move to New York to follow his dreams.[124] Within one year, he had performed at the Apollo Theatre in Harlem. From there, he would go on tour with Art Blakey's Messengers, and work with Roland Kirk and Mary Lou Williams. In the sixties, he began performing with the world renowned Count Basie. He was called to military service, completed his tour, and upon returning to music would perform for both Presidents Kennedy and Johnson at their inaugural balls.

Later, he would work with Pharoah Sanders, saxophonist and one of the fathers of 'free jazz' who played with and was mentored by jazz great, Johnny Coltrane. Pharoah Sanders and Leon Thomas would form their own sound which was developed from using African sounds and Eastern Meditation as influences. The two integrated Black Consciousness into their music. Sanders and Thomas wrote the song "The Creator has a Master Plan," which Thomas performed with Louis Armstrong on his work *Peace*. He and Sanders would later perform the song together.[125]

Sanders and Thomas symbolized the cutting edge of radical Black music and became major influences in jazz. Leon Thomas became known for a vocal technique that came to him by chance. Thomas and Sanders were to perform at a church, but due to an accident, Thomas had eight stitches in his mouth. Even with the injury, Sanders told Thomas that he could not pull out of the performance. Thomas says that when he went to scat, this great sound came out, called 'yodeling' by others, but Thomas named it 'Soularfone.' He said that it was a voice from the ancestors that arrived, a type of throat articulation. He was quoted as saying, "This voice is not me, my voice was ancient. The pygmies call it Umbo Weti. It surprises me, it does everything of its own volition."

In 1973, Carlos Santana wanted to tap into the energy that had been created by Sanders and Thomas. So he asked Thomas to come on tour with him. This has been considered to be the tour that established Santana as a major figure in the jazz scene. During the tour, Thomas served as the vocal lead and played a number of instruments. His performances were said to be astounding. He would appear on Santana's albums *Welcome* and *Lotus*. He would also release albums of his own on the Flying Dutchman Label:

Spirits Known and Unknown, I am Leon Thomas, Facets and others.

His career would suffer ups and downs due to drug usage. He released music sporadically. In 1988, he released a blues album on the Portrait label titled, *The Leon Thomas Blues Band.*[126] In the 90's, he returned to regularly perform at the famed Lenox Lounge in Harlem, New York. He would die in 1999, after recording an album with a small Indie label that was said to be some of his best work. Unfortunately, the album would not be released.

Leon Thomas revolutionized jazz music and was influenced by and influenced some of the greatest jazz musicians in history. Leon Thomas is a Legendary East St. Louisan.

Dr. LaRona Walls-Morris

"I feel that my greatest personal achievement centers around my being accepted as a friend of mankind."[127]

A native of East St. Louis and a product of East St. Louis Public Schools, Dr. LaRona J. Walls Morris would tirelessly serve her community. After graduating from East St. Louis Sr. High School, she received both her Bachelors in Business Education and her Master's in Counselor Education from Southern Illinois University in Edwardsville. Later while working full time, she and her sister, Dr. Stephanie Carpenter (a Legendary East St. Louisan in her own right)[128] would travel evenings after work to pursue their doctorate in Educational Administration and Higher Education from Southern Illinois University at Carbondale.[129] The women would often get home around 2:00 a.m. or later; then have to go back to work the next morning. They would diligently work in this manner until they completed their Doctorate degrees. Dr. Morris' educational achievements led to acceptance into Phi Delta Kappa, Pi Lambda Theta Honor Society.

Her community involvement was immeasurable including serving on the boards of the NAACP, the Girl Scouts, the Boy Scouts, and Big Brother/Big Sisters. She was also a member of Illinois Women Administrators, National Council of Negro Women, Business and Professional Women, the East St. Louis Principals Association, the American Institute of Parliamentarians, the Optimists, Order of the Eastern Star, and the Order of the Elks.

Moreover, Dr. Morris was a member of Sigma Gamma Rho Sorority and rose to become the 19th International Grand Basileus. She was the first East St. Louisan to serve as the head of a national sorority. While leading the organization, she implemented Operation Big Book Bag, a community service project that provided school supplies to disadvantaged youth in homeless shelters and crisis centers. She also initiated a nationwide adolescent youth symposium to help teens deal with peer pressure. Moreover, during her leadership, the Mwanimugimu (Wah-nah-moo-gee-moo) Essay Contest was implemented. The essay contest focuses on encouraging students to increase their knowledge of the historical and contemporary development of Africa. The prime objective of this project is to improve writing and research skills.[130]

As a torchbearer in the education field, she served as Special Assistant to the St. Clair County Regional Superintendent of Schools under Martha O'Malley, the first African-American to hold the position. She would go on to serve as assistant principal, and then principal at Wirth Jr. High School in Cahokia. After which, Morris was elected to the school board of District 189. She was a member of the team that facilitated many changes in the district. She chaired the School Uniform Committee and realized the adoption of the K-12 mandate for school uniforms. She also spearheaded the inclusion of JROTC in high schools. Although reelected, she would return to her first calling, school administration. She resigned as board member when offered a position as an assistant principal at her alma mater East St. Louis Sr. High. She would serve in many positions throughout the city including serving as Special Assistant to the first African American mayor, James Williams.

Because of her dedication and determination, Dr. Morris received over 150 Awards, including being listed as one of America's Most Influential African-Americans. She was featured in Jet, Ebony, and Black Enterprise Magazines. Upon her death, Senate Resolution SR0312 was written to commemorate her life.

Her words say it best, "If East St. Louis is to grow and prosper, it is believed that we, as citizens, must become more involved and more interested in those processes that govern and decide the destiny of our future as a productive city."

Dr. LaRona J. Wall-Morris, a visionary, a leader, a pioneer in education and most of all a servant to her community. Dr. Morris is a Legendary East St. Louisan.

Dr. Henri H. Weathers Jr.

Photo Credit: Ebony Tree

Weathers dedication to the city proves that you do not have to be born in a town for that place to be your HOMEtown.

Though a native of Rolling Fork, Mississippi, Dr. Henri Weathers Jr. chose East Saint Louis as the perfect place for his medical practice and his home.[131] A graduate of Fisk University and a member of Alpha Phi Alpha Fraternity, he would graduate from Meharry Medical School in 1927. Meharry Medical School was the first Southern medical school which accepted African Americans; it is one of the nation's oldest and largest historically Black educational institutions.

Once here in East St. Louis, he proved a valuable member of the community. Weathers fought alongside other prominent

African American doctors to have the St. Clair County Medical Society to allow African American doctors membership.[132] Without membership, they were not allowed to join other national organizations and more importantly were not allowed to be employed by government facilities.

Ultimately, Weathers would become a member of St. Clair Medical Society, the American College of Surgeons and International College of Surgeons. He gained worldwide attention, when he performed a successful surgery on the heart early in his career when most in the medical profession still considered the heart too fragile to operate on.

Though he died an early death at the age of 47, he was regarded as an esteemed doctor, and a valuable member of the community. Dr. Weathers was one of a group of three African-Americans hired by Saint Louis University Medical School as the first African American professors. He was chief of surgery at St. Mary's Infirmary in St. Louis and at St. Mary's Hospital in East St. Louis.

Moreover, he ran a successful private medical practice. The Orr Weathers public housing building is named for him, as it was built at 1300 Missouri Ave– the former location of his practice.[133] Dr. Weathers died in August of 1950. Because he was so beloved by his community, it is estimated that 15,000 people attended his wake. This estimate was posted in the *Crusader* newspaper. His funeral was held at St. Luke A.M.E, but the church could not hold all of the mourners. Almost 5,000 mourners stood outside in pouring rain to pay their respects because the church was full.[134]

Weathers was a Legendary East St. Louisan whose dedication to the city proved that you do not have to be born in a town for that place to be your HOMEtown.

Judge Milton S. Wharton

Photo Credit: ESLNAACP.org

A judge who led with respect for all; thus, he earned the respect of others.

In the sixty's, Milton S. Wharton lost his job as a welder due to layoffs. At the time, with little prospects of going back to his job, he decided that he should explore going to school. He decided to enroll at Southern Illinois University at Edwardsville (SIUE), and would go on to graduate in 1969 with a B.S. in Business Administration from SIUE. He then went to DePaul University and graduated with a law degree in 1975.[135] In 1976, he was appointed associate judge for St. Clair County, becoming one of the only African American Circuit Court Judges in Southern Illinois.

He served as a juvenile court judge and an adult court judge. Though he would become known for his work in the adult courts, trying high-profile cases such as the Chris Coleman case which had become the subject of nationwide outrage – Coleman had been accused and later convicted of killing his wife and two children. Speaking to the St. Louis Post-Dispatch, he expressed how fulfilling it had been to be a juvenile court judge.[136] Judge Wharton stated that he often still received thank you notes from men who had been juveniles before him in court and had changed their lives due to his guidance. He was known to be kind to everyone before him, lawyers and defendants alike. Noted as a fair judge, he gave speeches to young men, often young African American men from his native East St. Louis about steering clear of crime, and taking their life down more positive paths.

In 2010, he was entered into the SIUE Alumni Hall of Fame. At the time of his speech, he had been on the bench for more than 33 years, working for free beyond his date of expected retirement, was the President of the St. Clair County Bar Association, had been awarded numerous awards for community service; yet, he felt that he was undeserving of being in the Hall of Fame. In his acceptance speech, he spoke not of himself, but of the growing amount of African American males that were in jail in the State of Illinois. He called this fact "tragic and unacceptable." He further stated that everyone needed to come together and address the inequities between young African-Americans and Caucasians. Though he felt that the award was undeserved, he "would take it with the recognition that with it comes the responsibility to do more. To try to help more people."[137]

By the time he retired in 2012, he had served on the bench for over 35 years. He had received innumerable awards, among them, the Kimmel Community Service Award, the Martin Luther King Humanitarian Award, Whitney E. Young, Jr. Service Award of the Boy Scouts of America, and the Legend in the Legal Community Award from the *Argus* Newspaper. Furthermore, he had received the Pro Ecclesia Et Pontifice[138] from the late Pope John Paul II; this award is the highest level award conferred to those who are not clergy for their service to society.

The Honorable Milton Wharton went from welder, to business student, to law student to visionary judge. A judge who led with respect for all; thus, he earned the respect of others. He was a rarity in his field, a judge who led the charge against a society which would stand by idly while large percentages of African American men were being incarcerated. He chose to not just stand by. He chose to make a difference. Judge Milton Wharton is an asset to his community, and he is a Legendary East St. Louisan.

Judge Donald Wilkerson

Photo Credit: estlfund.org

Former Educator Teaches us about Pursuing Our Dreams

Judge Donald Wilkerson's story is one of autonomy, perseverance, but most of all service. His achievement is a testament that it is never too late to pursue your dreams.   A native East St. Louisan, Wilkerson completed an undergraduate degree from Illinois State University in Political Science. He would then graduate from Southern Illinois University in Edwardsville with a Master's in Education.

After receiving his Master's, he began teaching and coaching for East St. Louis School District 189. At one time, teaching math at the original Clark Junior High School at 3310 State St. He would spend 17 years educating and inspiring the youth, and while teaching, one student would return the favor. In an interview with the *St. Louis American,* Wilkerson stated that he always wanted to practice law. Then, ""One day a student asked me, 'Why don't you do it?' I didn't have an answer. I'd have to say that was my inspiration."[1]

He enrolled in an evening law program at St. Louis University and began juggling school on two fronts – as both a teacher and a student. In 1993, 20 years after receiving his undergraduate degree, he graduated from the evening program of St. Louis University School of Law (cum laude).[139]

After graduating, he began to practice law at the Thomas Mitchell Law Firm in St. Louis and later Stolar Partnership Law Firm. By 1995, he was appointed as Assistant U. S. Attorney for the Eastern District of Missouri. After only ten years as a U.S. Attorney, on January 4, 2005, Wilkerson was the first minority ever to be appointed to the bench in the Southern District of Illinois. His courtroom is located in East St. Louis.

Wilkerson says that his appointment is important not only in judicial circles, but also because "all public institutions should reflect the makeup of the entire community. It gives the community at large more confidence in the institution. Without confidence, the institution cannot exist."[140]

Judge Donald Wilkerson was reappointed to the bench for another eight-year term on January 4th 2013. Thus, he continues to serve his hometown. Wilkerson is correct that his appointment is important because he serves as a representative of the community;

but his appointment is also important because it teaches us that when we pursue our dreams anything is possible. He is an inspiration and a Legendary East St. Louisan.

James Williams Jr.

James Williams Jr. has been called a Lieutenant, the McDonald's man, a millionaire and a successful businessman.

At the age of 16, just like any other teenager, James Williams started his first job working at the local McDonald's restaurant. However, his experience would prove to be different than the typical teenagers. Williams was able to learn life lessons from Dr. Ben Davis, the owner of the McDonald's in his hometown of East St. Louis. His experience there would never be forgotten.[141]

After high school, Williams, the son of James Williams Sr. (the first African American Mayor of East St. Louis), would go to Dickenson College in Pennsylvania to major in Political Science. After college, he would pursue a career as a Navy pilot, but his experiences as a teen at McDonald's would still play an important role in his life. By chance, while stationed in San Diego, Williams would run into three businessmen from St. Louis; Ray Korte, Pete Nikolaisen, and Sam Temperato.[142] Williams would discuss with them his aspirations to own a McDonald's. This chance meeting would lead to another career. Nikolaisen, the founder of Luigi's Restaurant and Frozen Pizza Inc., would help Williams to write a letter to the CEO of McDonald's. Inside of the letter, they would put a picture of Williams climbing into the cockpit of a plane. Just like that, Williams was in. Within two years of entering the owner's training program, Williams would buy a McDonald's in Granite City.

Now, Williams' company Estel Foods, Inc., based in East St. Louis, owns 12 McDonald's throughout the Metro area. He, just as Dr. Davis, works in the McDonald's, and considers himself and the employees a team. According to him, his proudest purchase was the 2013 purchase of the McDonald's in East St. Louis. In a speech, while presenting an Academic Excellence Award Scholarship, he said that the decision to buy the location was a business decision, but it was also personal. "It's good to do business in East St. Louis...I grew up right down the street, and it's extremely personal... and it's going to be the best McDonald's in the area."[143]

Besides fulfilling his dream of becoming an entrepreneur, he also gives back to the community. He has donated his time to several organizations. He was a board member at the Jackie Joyner-Kersee Foundation, the East St. Louis Library, and the

Ronald McDonald Foundation. He volunteers his time to Archways to Opportunity, a program that supports youth furthering their education– seeking a GED, learning English as a Second Language, or preparing for college. He also donates his time to Boy Scouts of America and the Boys & Girls Club of Greater St. Louis.

Michael McMillan, President of the Urban League of Metropolitan St. Louis and former license collector and alderman in St. Louis, said it best when Williams was opening a McDonald's in St. Louis, "It's very significant for the minority business community to have an African-American owner making this multi-million-dollar investment in the downtown area," It sets an example to all young people and city residents in the community of what can be done by black business people."

James Williams has been called a Lieutenant, the McDonald's man, a millionaire and a successful businessman. We will call him an inspiration and a Legendary East St. Louisan.

Staci Yandle

An Exemplary Legal Mind, a Leader in the LGBT Community

In January of 2014, Barack Obama nominated Staci Yandle to be a United States District Judge for the Southern District of Illinois. If appointed, she would be the first African-American female, and the first openly LGBT Judge in the State of Illinois. Yandle is a native East St. Louisan (by way of Centreville), who upon graduation from Assumption High School[144] completed her undergraduate studies at the University of Illinois at Urbana-Champaign.[145] From there, she would earn her Juris Doctorate from Vanderbilt University School of Law in 1987. While in college, she would set out on a course to distinguish herself amongst her peers. In the Summer of 1984, she would serve as a Law Clerk for the Illinois Attorney General's Office. She would serve as Law Clerk again in '86 and '87. In '85, she would Intern for The Vanderbilt Legal Clinic and in '87 she would Intern at the Madison County Circuit Court for Judge Charles Chapman.

Upon graduation, she would work for several Law Firms, including Rex Carr Law Firm in East St. Louis, IL, before starting her own practice in 2007– The Law Offices of Staci M. Yandle. Senator Dick Durbin, a fellow East St. Louisan, said that he recommended Yandle for a judgeship because she fights for the little guy. This fight for the little guy can be seen not only in her court cases, but in her service. Yandle has donated her time to several organizations including – The American Association for Justice, Jackie Joyner-Kersee Foundation, Illinois Bar Foundation, Southend Development Corporation, Blacks Assisting Blacks Against AIDS, the NAACP and serval others.[146]

For her distinguished service, she has received numerous awards. Among them was the 2006, 2010 and 2011 Distinguished Service Award from the American Association for Justice. In 2012, she received the Women's Trial Lawyers Caucus, Marie Lambert Award, which is given in recognition of exemplary leadership to the profession, to her community, to AAJ, and to the Women Trial Lawyers Caucus.[147] In 2013, she received the Racial Harmony, Phenomenal Women of Metropolitan St. Louis Award. Awardees are defined by the organization as people who "step by step and bit by bit, have made an impact on changing our world."[148]

She has received a host of other awards and honors from several organizations including – National Council of Negro Women, Delta Sigma Theta, and the Jackie Joyner-Kersee Foundation.

However, her highest honor would come on August 22, 2014, when she was appointed by Barack Obama as United States District Judge for the Southern District of Illinois. Her appointment would prove a success for African-Americans, the LBGT community, and East St. Louisans. Senator Durbin said of her appointment, ""In short, Staci Yandle's confirmation marks another important milestone in the journey toward equality of opportunity for all Americans."[149]

Judge Stacy Yandle an exemplary legal mind, a first in the State of Illinois, and a Legendary East St. Louisan.

Afterward

I put a feeler on Facebook to try to find younger people for the book. It said something like, if you know any prominent young people from East St. Louis contact me…. A response on the post asked, "What is your definition of Prominent?" It was a great question. There are so many people who have achieved greatness from East St. Louis, and who continue to achieve greatness every day.

This greatness can be found in the local school teacher who sparks the interest and intellect of his or her pupils as Dr. Redmond said of his teacher who sparked his intrigue of literature. It is in the parents who dutifully raise and nurture their children and encourage them in their dreams like the Hudlins or Diane Bolden-Taylor. It can be found in the neighborhood Pharmacist, Buchannan, or former mayor William Mason* who choose to serve their hometown for their entire life. It can be found in the firsts like Dr. Weathers, or the bests like Jackie Joyner-Kersee and Al Joyner.

These people weren't born exceptional or great, they created their own form of greatness. They figured out what they wanted to do, and they went about doing it. They worked hard, and found some doors closed to them, but they persevered. They excelled in spite of or maybe because of the trials they were faced with; and that's what makes them and their lives great and their stories inspirational. They inspire us to want to be great. Reading their stories makes the reader feel as if he can reach through an ethereal film and grab hold to the magic that resonates in all of their experiences. Their stories transcend a town, or even a race, and exemplify the greatness that lies dormant in all of us. It speaks to us, "Find your greatness."

Tiffany Lee

Note: We would like to say that this book is in no way meant to be a comprehensive look at a group of people whose resilience and dedication could never be fully explained or contained within one work. Rather, it is an attempt to give an inspirational look at a few people from the African American population of East St. Louis, who have overcome racism, poverty, and (possibly the worst of all) stereotypical perceptions.

Many of the older profiles are people who are not 'from' East St. Louis, but they are of the generation that came from the South and helped to build the African American community in East St. Louis.

Appendix

This is an addendum to Henri Weathers Profile: Letter from Dr. Henri Weathers to W.E.B Dubois about their Fraternity.

MEDICINE
DENTISTRY

FORTY-SIXTH YEAR
OVER THREE THOUSAND GRADUATES

PHARMACY
NURSE-TRAINING

Meharry Medical College
Nashville, Tennessee

Nov. 23, 1924.

Dr. W. E. B. Du Bois,
Editor of the Crisis
New York City.

Dear Brother Du Bois,

Doubtless, you have heard of the recent occurrences at our Alma Mater (Fisk). For that reason I shall make no attempt to tell you of said occurrences, however I am coming to you for a bit of advice.

In spite of the indefinite reply given by the Trustees in response to the grievances and requests of the student body over at Fisk, our chapter (Chi) has been besieged with applications for membership into Alpha Phi Alpha. Naturally the fraternity asks me for advice concerning the manner since I am a graduate of Fisk.

Can you offer any suggestion concerning what disposal should be made of Fisk applicants for membership? Is it wise to accept Fisk men into Alpha in view of existing conditions?

This letter is of a personal nature, asking for advice in order that I may make recommendation and suggestion, and does not come from the fraternity.

Fraternally yours,
Henri W. Weathers,

This file is an addendum to the profile on Judge Billy Jones who helped to integrate the schools.

About the Author: Doris Robinson-Ellington was enrolled at East St. Louis Senior High School during this "first" attempt at integration in East St. Louis. Presently, she is a registered nurse residing in East St. Louis.

(These are notes listed on the original document. It is unknown the origin of this document.)

INTEGRATION OF SCHOOLS

By Doris Robinson-Ellington

Situated in an obscure part of town, cut off from the rest of the city by railroad tracks, and surrounded by stock yards and meat packing companies was a unique section of East St. Louis called Goose Hill. Locked in the boundary lines of that unique little neighborhood was a people, a Black people filled with hope, faith, dreams, desires and ambitions that were festering within their hearts and minds like the hot lava in a volcano that was about to erupt. Most of the inhabitants of that neighborhood were immigrants from the South, who brought along with them to the North the warm and friendly customs not practiced by most of their city sisters and brothers of color. They were not merely friends and neighbors but family, sharing and supporting each other.

Within that neighborhood was a confectionary located on the corner of Second Street and Bowman Avenue. It was owned and operated by Mr. Robert Perry Storman and was fittingly called Perry's. This corner served as a meeting place for many of the neighborhood youths who played ball for Mr. Storman. A daily exchange of ideas and plans for the future, some of which sounded like pipe dreams, was shared at that location.

It was there at that location around a pot-bellied coal heater in the year 1948 that the idea of school integration was born and implanted into the minds of some of the youngsters who lived on Goose Hill. Richard Taylor and Otis Garrett were present when Mr. Storman stated that, when his daughter Delois completed the eighth grade at Carver School, his plan was to enroll her at Rock Jr. High, an all-white school much closer to his home than Lincoln High, the all Black school across town. Little did Mr. Storman know that his thoughts of school integration were right on time because chapters of the NAACP were forming protest groups across the nation to vocalize racial unrest over the discriminatory practices against America's black people.

Foreseeing possible problems and resistance against his plan, Mr. Storman enlisted the support of the local N.A.A.C.P., its president Mr. David Owens, and board members Norvell Hickman and Attorney Billy Jones. On January 31, 1949, these men, along with Mr. Storman, formed a delegation and demanded the registration of seven Black students at East St. Louis Senior High and fourteen at the Rock Jr. High. On the

First day of attempt the students were led to an empty room where they were left unattended all day. At the end of the day the students and delegation were told by the principals of those schools that no new registrations were being accepted pending directions by the Board of Education. February 1, 1949, the same delegation of students led by Mr. Storm and Attorney Billy Jones appeared for the second day seeking admission to the schools.

I am certain many white organizational meeting had been held the evening before to plan actions to be taken against any further attempts to enroll Black students in the white system. A potentially dangerous scenario developed in February when the bell rang for the first class and word circulated throughout the classrooms that there were black students in the schools. Several hundred white youngsters led by teachers formed a picket line and marched around the two adjoining schools waving banners and picket signs imprinted with derogatory racial slurs and inflammatory inscriptions. Whited parents gathered on the sidewalks outside the school and joined the students in protest. Hundreds of other white students marched through the downtown section of town ending up at City Hall, demanding that the Sheriff's Department go over and put the black students out of their school.

On that day demonstrations and protest marches popped up all over town almost simultaneously. A white group called the Progressive Party formed a Freedom Day demonstration at the Board of Education in support of the board's refusal to admit the Black students. Not one group came out in support of the black students other than the group headed by Mr. Storman. Meeting after meeting was held. The school board met several times in one day in gatherings that were termed, by the board president Bernice Goode, as informal meetings. These informal meetings excluded the one Black member of the board. The lone black member, Mr. Marion Stallings, Sr., was present at only one of those meetings. When he made a motion that the Black students be admitted, his motion, of course, died on the floor for the want of a second.

Up to this point in our history as American blacks, our strongest organization was the church, but ironically several of the city's best-known ministers from the Sound End rejected the move to enroll black students in white schools, describing the attempt as a "rash act and a serious blunder which might do something to close the doors of opportunity in our faces." The same as always, the white man's strategic efforts were working: "Divide and Conquer." Only this time we were not a combined body to separate. That very small number of Goose Hillers stood alone, but they stood together as they had from the start and the determination of Perry Storman to accomplish his dream would soon become a reality.

The leaders sensed that violence was brewing and became concerned about the safety of the children. Therefore, after four non-productive days the children were withdrawn from the schools, and Lawyer Billy Jones filed what may have been the first lawsuit in the country to integrate public schools. A year later the Court of Appeals ruled in favor of the children, and on January 31, 1950, one hundred black students were admitted to six schools that previously had been attended by white students only.

14 Cannady Elementary

17 Rock Jr. High

21 East St. Louis Sr. High

28 Webster Elementary School

05 Monroe Elementary School

15 Alta Sita Elementary School

At Franklin Elementary School, which had been all black, two white students enrolled. This momentous occasion, which effectively integrated all the public schools in Southern Illinois, occurred years before the nationally renowned case of Brown vs. Topeka Kansas Board of Education, decided by the U. S. Supreme Court in 1954.

I was in that number at East St. Louis High School and needless to say, it was not easy. However, most of those students did the black race proudly. They were all high achievers in every aspect of the word. Practically all at the high school came from roots deeply embedded in the Southern Mission Missionary Baptist Church, which was at that time located on "Goose Hill." Wardell Brooks our first black graduate, set a typing speed record of more than one hundred words per minute his on one and only semester at E. St. Louis High. Mr. Brooks is now the Director of Housing, in Waukegan, Illinois, and owner and operator of the day care center. Richard Taylor and Ronal Mitchell set track and field records, not only in this region but statewide. Mr. Taylor is now an administrator

For District 189. Dennis Perry and Delores Storman Ray were our first black students to be inducted into the National Honor Society. Mrs. Ray is presently the Director of Mental Health, St. Clair County. Mr. Perry is Professor of Microbiology at Northwestern University. Mr. Gus Doss, who was very impressive in basketball, is now assistant principal and athletic director at Custer High School, one of Milwaukee, Wisconsin's largest. Thomas Little, graduated with honors and is now a successful practicing attorney in an East Coast city. Louie Williams, all city athlete, is now a minister and administrator with School District 189. Valletta Smith Howse is a nurse in Springfield, Illinois. Mary Granger-Sims, honor student, now top in sales at Sears, Roebuck and Company. I am a registered nurse at Barnes Hospital. Many teachers of the Carver School family, such as Earlie Knockum Foggy, Alfrenia Yong Hampton, Vera Bates Washington, John DeShields, John Williams, Ocie Bailey and Helen Wren Brown, are owed a vote of thanks for their dedication and expertise in preparing and equipping those students with good scholastic backgrounds and the self-esteem that was necessary to face those bleak days of the 50's. Many of us have the man with a vision, Mr. Storman, to thank for where we are in our careers today.

This file is an addendum to the profile on John Robinson who fought for schools for African American Children. The original document was found in the *Ebony Tree*.

A PLACE CALLED LINCOLN

600 N. 6th Street   1906 – 1911

1000 N. Broadway   1911 – 1950

1211 Bond Ave.   1950 – 1998

HISTORY OF LINCOLN HIGH SCHOOL
EAST ST. LOUIS, ILLINOIS

WRITTEN BY MISS LUCY MAE TURNER, from information gained as a teacher in the school for twenty years, from consultation with Mrs. Dorothy Hawkins-Hickman and Miss Fannie J. Jones, who attended this school in their early years, and from reading the historical files of the Board of Education.

In the middle of April, 1911, Lincoln High School, at the corner of Tenth Street and Broadway, East St. Louis, was alive with activity. The principal, Mr. Benjamin Franklin Bowles, was happy and successful and satisfied with his position as head of the Lincoln Polytechnic High School.

The eighteen teachers in the building were: 1. Mr. Bowles, the principal, 2. Miss Minnie Scott, the head teacher, 3. Miss Daisy West-brooks, music and typing, 4. Mrs. Casey Grady, domestic science, 5. Mr. Orestes Hood, manual training, electricity and plumbing, 6. Mr. Charles Scholls, 7. Miss Maude Kennedy, 8. Miss Blanch Nichols, 9. Miss Emma Edwards (who later married Undertaker Nash, and became the mother of Claudia, Fredericka, and Frances), 10. Miss Jean Hamilton, 11. Miss Idella Phillips (now Mrs. Ed. Williams of Edwardsville, Ill.), 12. Miss Georgianna Charleston, 13. Miss Cora Westbrooks, 14. Miss Ida Gee, 15. Miss Sophronia Day, 16. Miss Ella Day, 17. Mrs. Denelits, 18. Miss Sadie Buster.

Mr. Bowles, besides serving as principal, had organized a creditable school band, and personally instructed the pupils in the use of the different instruments. Mr. John Eubanks, senior, who was very young and active in those days, often as an interested parent, lent Mr. Bowles assistance with the band, as his two young sons, John and Horace, were being trained in it. The later famous orchestra leader, Charles Creaty, was trained in Mr. Bowles' orchestra.

But, in April, 1911, Mr. Charles Scholls, whose home was in St. Louis, Missouri, was suffering from some incurable disease, and was just staying at school long enough to pass over his room and his records to Miss Lucy Mae Turner, from Zanesville, Ohio, who had recently graduated from Wilberforce University. In those days, before you could be a regular teacher in East St. Louis, you had to serve two years as a substitute teacher, or have two years' experience elsewhere. Therefore, when I came to East St. Louis, I had taught one year in Paducah, Kentucky, and one year in Sisterville, West Virginia.

I arrived that morning in April, 1911 (I believe it was Wednesday) on the 9:00 a.m. Baltimore and Ohio Train, and was met by Mr. Bowles who took me at once to the school. We walked from the Relay Depot to the school at Tenth Street and Broadway. Automobiles were so scarce in those days that the only colored family in town that had one was the family of Attorney Parden, the father of Mrs. Lillian Bracey.

In the year 1911, colored schools had been in East St. Louis for forty-one years, as historic files record that the first colored school was conducted in the Baptist Church (presumably Macedonia) on Brady Avenue, in the year 1871. Mr. Frances Moss is named as the first teacher.

The colored school was conducted in various places at various times. One of the places mentioned most frequently is the BLACKSMITH SHOP, down below Broadway. Now, when I arrived in 1911, the A.M.E. Zion Church and a blacksmith shop were located on Rock Road, just off of Broadway, and I have an unconfirmed idea that that is where the colored school was held.

Well, things rocked on from 1871 till 1886, when three Godly-inspired men got sick at soul of the inconvenience and injustice being put upon their people and their children in seeking to obtain an education. Captain John Robinson had been a slave in the deep south. Also, by some means, he had fought with the Union Army in the Civil War. Captain Robinson thought that if people of his color were good enough to fight and die for this country alongside the whiter-skinned Americans, then, their children were good enough to sit beside other American children, of lighter skin, and get an education.

The second of our patriots was Mr. Morton Hawkins, the grandfather of our present coroner, Norvel Hickman. Mr. Hawkins believed firmly in equality of voting rights and equality of educational rights. Although Morton Hawkins was kept quite busy at his job of running with the money to get the colored children dressed up and ready for their historic march from the blacksmith shop to their entry into the exclusive white school.

The third member of this race-loving and freedom-loving set was Mr. Beasley, a brother-in-law of Mr. Morton Hawkins. Mr. Beasley also ran on the railroad; nevertheless, Mr. Beasley also did his share in furnishing finance, help, and encouragement to Captain John Robinson in putting over his magnificent coup of leading the colored children from the delapi-dated blacksmith shop to the spacious and comfortable white school.

According to historic records, Captain John Robinson must have led the colored children to the Clay School, which was the name of the white school from 1883 till 1886. The Clay School was a large, two-story frame

Page Three
April 26, 1962

building at the southeast corner of Collinsville Avenue and St. Louis Avenue. The principals of the Clay School were Frank Rafter till 1884, and later Charles Manners.

Captain John Robinson's historic march was sometime in the early eighties. So nonplused and startled were the white parents when they saw colored children sitting in the seats with their lily-white offspring, that they immediately decided to build a school for the colored children whose number had increased so rapidly that a blacksmith shop was no longer able to hold them comfortably.

The colored school was finished in 1886, at the corner of Sixth Street and St. Louis Avenue, and was formerly called the Lincoln High School. Now, in 1962, the Board of Education Building, it was a combined elementary school and high school for Negroes, and was so conducted until 1909, when it was converted into permanent quarters for the Board of Education.

Another building was erected, and Lincoln High School was moved to a new location, at Tenth Street and Broadway in 1909.

Captain John Robinson died in 1918. I remember the last time I saw him. In 1917, they took one thousand colored men from East St. Louis to serve in the First World War. The citizens gave a big dance for the men at the old Judson Hall, later St. Luke Church, at Thirteenth Street and Broadway. The floor was so crowded that people stood shoulder to shoulder, so that there was hardly standing room, let alone dancing room. The piano groaned on (this was the day before big orchestras) and honestly, one could hardly tell whether the music was a ditty or a dirge.

Then, along about midnight, everybody marched on foot to the Relay Depot, to see the soldiers board the train. Some of the departing soldiers stood on top of the train as it moved off, to get a last long glimpse of their home and their loved ones.

Just before the soldiers and their friends left Judson Hall for the walk to the Relay Depot, Captain John Robinson climbed a twenty foot high balcony, at the front of the hall, spread above the crowd a large American flag which reached from the balcony nearly to the floor, and addressed the one thousand young men on their duties to their country, their race, and their God. It was indeed an inspiring moment. Captain John Robinson was a wonderful and dramatic orator.

The first Lincoln High School at Sixth Street and St. Louis Avenue served the colored people for twenty-three years, from 1886 till 1909. The first principal was Mr. Byron, able, well liked, and of great service to the community. Then came Mr. Thompson, who was removed by accidental death.

After Mr. Thompson came Mr. Benjamin Franklin Bowles, from Ohio, who served as principal of both the first Lincoln High at Sixth and St. Louis Avenue, and of the second Lincoln High at Tenth Street and Broadway.

The first graduating class from Sixth and St. Louis Avenue consisted of Minnie and Molly Scott, and Fannie Edwards, the aunt of Misses Claudia, Fredericka, and Frances Nash. I believe at that time, Mr. Byron was principal. Mrs. Dorothy Hawkins-Hickman graduated from Lincoln High School, Sixth and St. Louis Avenue, with Mr. Bowles as principal, in June, 1900.

The Hawkins' family home was near Sixth and St. Louis Avenue, across from the spot where the Ainad Temple now stands. The St. Luke A.M.E. Church was also near that same location in 1911. So Sixth and St. Louis Avenue was quite an important corner, with the Hawkins' home, the St. Luke A.M.E. Church, and the colored High School, all in the immediate vicinity.

When I arrived in East St. Louis in 1911, the only evening diversion was attending a Nickelodeon, which the Hawkins brothers, sons of Morton Hawkins, conducted on a sawdust-covered lot, about ten or fifteen feet below the sidewalk, on Broadway, where the Broadview Convalescent Center now stands. One of the Hawkins brothers carried the mail, and one in later years, started the Harlem Theater, on South Main Street.

Of course, movies were unknown in 1911, and a Nickelodeon just flashed a picture on a sheet, then off, while the music played. But the young minds of that day just thought it was great. The only talking machine was a Gramophone or Graphophone, with an enormous horn, like a band instrument, which could talk just a little.

Mr. Bowles, in 1909, moved as principal to the new Lincoln High School at Tenth Street and Broadway. In 1914, Mr. Bowles accepted a position at Lincoln University, Jefferson City, Missouri. He was replaced by Mr. John W. Hughes, from the principalship at Wheeling, West Virginia.

The school flourished under Mr. Hughes, and the enrollment far exceeded the capacity of the eighteen room building. When my sister, Miss Fannie V. Turner, came to teach at Lincoln in 1916, there were several portable school buildings in the yard, and a teacher would often look around and find that there wer over seventy children actually present in her room. So some wings were added to the Lincoln at Tenth and Broadway.

Mr. Hughes died at a ripe old age, in 1937, still serving as principal of Lincoln High School. Some time between 1930 and 1935, the grades below the Seventh, were taken from the Lincoln High School at Tenth and Broad-way, and placed in the John Robinson School at Fifteenth and Bond Avenue.

On Mr. Hughes' death in 1937, Mr. G. V. Quinn, an ex-soldier, be-came principal. Mr. G. V. Quinn served as principal until 1949, when he died quite unexpectedly, at the height of his career.

Mr. Ross Miller was elevated to the position of principal, and had the pleasure of moving into the present new Lincoln Building, on Twelfth Street and Bond Avenue. This building is fireproof, and quite modern, and was finished in 1950, after much planning and careful deliberation by the builders. Mr. Ross Miller served as Lincoln High School principal from 1949 till 1959, and under him, the Junior High School pupils were removed from the building, and Lincoln became really a Senior High School. In August, 1959, Mr. Miller was given a different position under the Board of Education, and Mr. Clifford W. Basfield, a graduate of Lincoln High School became Lincoln High School principal.

In this year, 1962, Mr. Basfield is still the very efficient principal of Lincoln High School at Twelfth and Bond Avenue.

The school has an enrollment of about twelve hundred pupils, a teach-ing staff of forty-nine, and, although there is some integration, Lincoln is rated as the largest colored High School in Southern Illinois.

THE END

[1] See more information in American Pogrom by Charles Lumpkins.
[2] Much of the information in this article was shared by Dr. Lillian Parks and written in the East St. Louis *Monitor*, unknown the date.
[3] Located at 2235 Bond Ave, East St. Louis
[4] Information gathered from the article, "Singer Finds Success Overseas" by Roger Schlueter in the *Belleville News Democrat*, date unknown.
[5] Information taken from her bio at http://www.loc.edu/documents/DrDianeBoldenBio.pdf
[6] Though in the first edition of this work, this information was referenced from the Post-Dispatch article listed in endnote four, changes to this bio were completed by Professor Bolden-Taylor.
[7] Information on faculty and Staff Bio for University of Northern Colorado: http://www.unco.edu/news/expertlist/index.aspx?id=175
[8] See Reginald Petty's files: 1903 East St. Louis Directory
[9] See *American Pogrom: The East St. Louis Race Riot and Black Politics*
[10] Page 136 in *Groping Towards Democracy: African American Social Welfare Reform in St. Louis*
[11] See more at: *Ebony Tree*
[12] See more at "Retirement is no Prescription for 92-year-old Pharmacist;" *St. Louis Post Dispatch*; 3 Jan. 05.
[13] Many of the players in Elwood's band would become national and international musicians, see more at *Miles Davis and American Culture*.
[14] Some sources have him as being born in St. Louis, but raised in East St. Louis. Unknown if he was just born in a hospital in St. Louis.
[15] Information taken from U.S. Department of State Page: http://www.state.gov/r/pa/ei/biog/225997.htm
[16] Information available from interview at http://www.thehistorymakers.com/biography/honorable-dwight-bush-sr
[17] An Introduction of himself as Ambassador can be located at https://www.youtube.com/watch?v=K9L9-mDUNcM
[18] See more at:http://www.nashfuneralhome.com/fh/obituaries/obituary.cfm?o_id=891379&fh_id=13211
[19] See more at: http://www.lwfaah.net/aaradio/part4.htm
[20] See more at: https://www.siue.edu/lovejoylibrary/musiclistening/NRJA/cheers.shtml
[21] See more in: *I Am EStL The Magazine*, March-April 2016, Sports Issue.
[22] See more in Sixty-Two Nationally Prominent East St. Louisans
[23] See more at: http://www.goleathernecks.com/hof.aspx?hof=45&path=&kiosk=
[24] See more at: http://www.thephinsider.com/2012/3/31/2907921/miami-dolphins-all-time-top-100-players-48-bryan-cox
[25] See more at: http://www.atlantafalcons.com/team/coaches/Bryan-Cox/56d2be68-0af9-4dc6-b289-764058381f8c
[26] See more at: http://fox2now.com/2013/07/09/bryan-cox-benefit-weekend/
[27] See more at: http://www.billboard.com/articles/columns/chart-beat/7401224/miles-davis-robert-glasper-everythings-beautiful-billboard-200-chart-moves, Robert Glasper reimagines Davis work on the album.

[28] See more in *Miles Davis and American Culture*
[29] See more at: http://www.biography.com/people/miles-davis-9267992#synopsis
[30] See more at: https://www.milesdavis.com/biography/
[31] Name is a nickname associated with Miles Davis.
[32] See more at: http://kdcah.org/, a KETC, Living St. Louis produced Anne-Marie Berger
[33] See more at: http://kdcah.org/katherine-dunham-biography/
[34] See more at: http://www.nytimes.com/1988/05/22/magazine/an-outsider-joins-the-team.html?pagewanted=all
[35] See more at: https://blogs.sjsu.edu/newsroom/2016/world-renowned-sports-sociologist-and-sjsu-alumnus-harry-edwards-to-serve-as-2016-commencement-speaker/
[36] "Harry Edwards." *Newsmakers*. Detroit: Gale, 1989. *Biography in Context*. Web. 11 May 2016.
[37] Edwards views on O.J.'s racial identity are further explored on http://www.richeisenshow.com/2016/06/15/uc-berkeley-professor-emeritus-dr-harry-edwards-weighs-in-on-espns-o-j-made-in-america-61516/
[38] Noted in one source as 1970 and another source as 1971.
[39] See more in *IAmEStL The Magazine* March-April 2016 Sports Issue
[40] Initially named the St. Louis Municipal Bridge, then renamed the Free Bridge, and later, the MacArthur Bridge after Douglass MacArthur. The bridge is currently no longer in use.
[41] Officer Mills and Officer nelson were also credited with either leading people away from mobs or sheltering people escaping the mobs.
[42] This information was found in *Power, Community, and Racial Killing in East St. Louis*; however, the testimony of John Eubanks Sr. can be seen on microfilm: 26 October 1917: Select Committee, pp.1146-1147 of transcripts of hearings (reel 2, frame 234, UPA microfilm collection). Also interesting article can be found at: http://blogs.democratandchronicle.com/rochesterarts2/?p=3300
[43] *The Ebony Tree*
[44] See more at: http://www.thepearlofomega.org/This-is-Alpha-Chapter-25
[45] See more at http://www.thehistorymakers.com/biography/larry-gladney-43
[46] See more at https://www.sas.upenn.edu/about/administration/gladney
[47] GS stands for general scale and is used for civilian government employees, scales run from 1-15.
[48] Much of the information concerning Mr. Grimmett was taken from his obituary, and http://www.afkapsi.com/docs/Golden%20Heritage%20Part%204.pdf as he is a life member of Kappa Alpha Psi Fraternity.
[49] See more at: http://cdharperbooks.com/?page_id=6
[50] It should be noted that he possesses a Certificate in Black Studies from the University of Wisconsin-Madison.
[51] These are exact words taken from his website, but cannot be attributed as a direct quote.
[52] *Belleville News-Democrat* "East St. Louis' Next Olympian" July 15, 2008
[53] See more at: http://fox2now.com/2012/10/04/parade-planned-for-olympian-dawn-harper/
[54] See more at http://www.dawnharpernelson.com/bio.html#myAnchor
[55] See more

at:http://www.stlamerican.com/salute_to_excellence/education_gala/article_f4288f6c-1857-11e4-bf92-001a4bcf887a.html

[56] *Ebony Tree*

[57] Reginald's Petty Files

[58] See more at http://www.stlamerican.com/news/obituaries/article_bef139e2-85b2-5da6-8b11-ba03ab4ad885.html

[59] See more at http://www.stltoday.com/news/local/metro/john-h-hicks-first-black-reporter-at-the-st-louis/article_7cd1ba24-2fa7-5072-9858-888cde0f56dd.html all other articles on Hicks reference this article.

[60] *African Americans in Science, Math and Invention*

[61] There are conflicting dates on this. Chemheritage.org lists this date as 1953, while *African Americans in Science, Math and Invention* lists this date as 1950.

[62] http://www.washingtonpost.com/wp-dyn/content/article/2005/09/23/AR2005092301919.html

[63] See more at: http://hudlinentertainment.com/about-me/the-reginald-hudlin-story/

[64] See more at: www.unewsonline.com/2002/02/21/archivesfeaturesexhibitonblackfamilies/

[65] See more at: http://www.dvrepublic.com/view.php?sid=1

[66] See more at: http://www.nytimes.com/1994/11/08/arts/television-review-moving-into-a-new-venue.html

[67] See more at: http://sports.yahoo.com/mma/news?slug=dm-ironring041108

[67] http://www.biography.com/people/jackie-joyner-kersee-9358710#personal-life

[68] Information in this article taken from Reginald Petty Files.

[69] Ebony Tree: Jones was a member of Alpha Kappa Mu Honor Society, the debate team, the Forensic Society and several other groups.

[70] See Howard University website: http://www.law.howard.edu/246

[71] See *Discovering African American St. Louis: A guide to Historic Sites* by Dr. John Wright

[72] See Appendix for story by Doris Robinson-Ellington

[73] https://www.usatf.org/HallOfFame/TF/showBio.asp?HOFIDs=201

[74] http://www.stltoday.com/news/local/metro/joyner-kersee-isn-t-giving-up-on-center-bearing-her/article_249ce674-4601-5eff-9ba3-0696c405f1a2.html

[75] http://www.biography.com/people/jackie-joyner-kersee-9358710#personal-life

[76] There were some papers before the Crusader, the Citizen

[77] *The Ebony Tree*

[78] Photo was taken in March 11th, 1965 and is a part of the Lyndon B Johnson Library.

[79] See more in *Jet Magazine* article published on March 16, 1972.

[80] Reginald Petty's files

[81] *Jet Magazine*, March 9, 1967 Publication

[82] *Jet* article

[83] Ebony Tree has the date listed as 1910. So does *American Pogrom*. Dr. Wrights work *Discovering African American St. Louis* has the date listed as some time in the 20's. One must remember that much of African-American History has been passed down orally: information conveyed through speaking. This often leads to minute details being lost or confused.

[84] See more at http://www.allmusic.com/artist/brother-joe-may-mn0000937715/biography

85 Bill Nunes, Sixty-Two Nationally Prominent East St. Louisans
86 See more at: https://news.illinoisstate.edu/2013/07/partner-to-presidents-donald-mchenrys-diplomatic-career/
87 See more at:
http://illinoisreview.typepad.com/illinoisreview/2006/10/illinois_hall_o_16.html
another source, Georgetown, has the degree as International Affairs.
88 *The Crisis*, November 1979
89 *I AM EStL The Magazine*, January-February 2016, Public Servants issue
90 See more at: https://isd.georgetown.edu/mchenry
91 See more at: http://www.coca-colacompany.com/press-center/press-releases/donald-f-mchenry-jacob-wallenberg-to-retire-from-the-coca-cola-company-board-of-directors

92 Reginald Petty's files, full names unknown, the majority of this information was taken from the website of the East St. Louis Chapter of the NAACP.
93 See more at:
http://www.nashfuneralhome.com/fh/obituaries/obituary.cfm?o_id=891483&fh_id=13211
94 See more at:
http://www.nashfuneralhome.com/fh/aboutus/history.cfm?&fh_id=13211
95 See more at:
http://www.nashfuneralhome.com/fh/aboutus/history.cfm?page=5&fh_id=13211
96 See more: Belleville News Democrat, Fredericka Nash Dies at 90..., 04 Apr. 2010
97 *The Ebony Tree*
98 See more at: http://www.officerfh.com/?page=aboutus
99 See more at: http://eslnaacp.org/salute.html
100 See more in *St. Louis Post-Dispatch* Obituary, February 11, 1989
101 "E. St. Louis Board Likes New Chief," *Saint Louis Post Dispatch*.
102 This quote is from *Savage Inequalities: Children in America's School* page 41.
103 St. Louis Post dispatch article: School Superintendent Quits in east St. Louis
104 *Sixty-Two Nationally Prominent East St. Louisans* by Bill Nunes
105 Most of the information for this article was taken from her obituary at http://www.legacy.com/obituaries/washingtonpost/obituary.aspx?pid=144888429

106 East St. Louis *Monitor*. "Monitoring the News." Eugene Redmond. July 27, 1967.
107 See more at: http://www.stltoday.com/news/local/education/east-st-louis-poet-and-pack-rat-collector-becomes-study/article_cafe7aa5-4fa2-5b89-a7bb-a252710dbae8.html
108 See more at: http://eugenebredmond.com/home/tag/poet-eugene-b-redmond/
Correction to date made by Dr. Redmond.
109 See more at: http://eugenebredmond.com/home/biography/

110 Information found in Reginald Petty's Files
111 Captain is believed to be a moniker given to him by the community due to his love for the military. It is not known his actual rank in the military.
112 *American Pogrom* listed Captain Robinson as a Civil War Veteran.

113 *The Ebony Tree*
114 *The Ebony Tree* has him listed as dying in 1918, but the East Saint Louis Daily Journal in a 1924 article has him listed as dying in 1919.
115 See more at:
http://www.nashfuneralhome.com/fh/aboutus/staff_member.cfm?stf_id=16167&fh_id=13211
116 Information on Reverend Scott available on the older website of NAACP, East St. Louis Chapter.
117 The Senator's wife, Loretta Durbin
118 See more at http://capitolwords.org/date/2013/01/24/S274-3_tribute-to-rev-johnny-scott/
119 Reginald Petty's Files
120 Information on *New York Times* website:
http://www.nytimes.com/2008/07/25/theater/25teer.html?_r=0
121 Information referenced from the theater's website: nationalblacktheatre.org
122 Best known for "Night Train" a number one single that stayed on the tracks for several weeks.
123 Jazz Guitarist
124 See more at: http://www.independent.co.uk/arts-entertainment/obituary-leon-thomas-1097568.html
125 See more at:
http://www.freeform.org/music/jazzsupreme/leon.thomas/santana.html
126 See more at http://www.allmusic.com/artist/leon-thomas-mn0000201515/biography

127 *Black Women Role Models of Greater St. Louis* by Dr. Sheryl Clayton, all quotes were taken from this work.
128 Dr. Stephanie Carpenter served for many years in district 189 as a dedicated teacher, principal, and assistant superintendent.
129 See more at: http://www.greekchat.com/gcforums/archive/index.php/t-68388.html
130 https://www.k-state.edu/sgrho/projects/
131 The Ebony Tree
132 American Pogrom
133 Discovering African American St. Louis: A Guide to Historic Sites by John Aaron Wright
134 Reginald Petty's files
135 See more at: https://www.siue.edu/business/alumni/wharton.shtml
136 See More at: http://www.stltoday.com/news/local/judge-milton-wharton-to-leave-bench/article_6f974c40-0403-11e1-8be3-0019bb30f31a.html
137 See more at: https://www.siue.edu/business/alumni/wharton.shtml
138 Latin for the Church and the Pope

139 Information taken from article in "Madison – St. Clair Record"
http://madisonrecord.com/stories/510573875-wilkerson-reappointed-magistrate-judge-in-sdil
140This Quote taken from online article: "**Judge Wilkerson Worked Way to Judicial History**" http://www.stlamerican.com/news/local_news/article_dc6aebde-466a-5349-

bb9c-5db1a4ca1e78.html

[141] See more at: http://www.stlamerican.com/business/article_d977f880-2bac-11e3-9177-001a4bcf887a.html

[142] See more in *Saint Louis Business Journal*, April 15-21, 2016; Vol.36, NO 35

[143] See more at: https://www.youtube.com/watch?v=FKas8AMTkc0

[144] A private high School in East St. Louis. Closed. Formally located at the corner of Kingshighway and Route 111.

[145] Information obtained from U.S. District Court Page:
http://www.ilsd.uscourts.gov/Judges/Yandle.aspx

[146] Information available via her application for judgeship at
http://www.judiciary.senate.gov/imo/media/doc/Staci-Yandle-Senate-Questionnaire-Final.pdf

[147] See more at: https://www.justice.org/what-we-do/enhance-practice-law/professional-recognition-awards-scholarship/awards/caucus-awards-1#sthash.al011emz.dpufn

[148] See more at centerforracialharmony.org

[149] Information from news article at
https://www.washingtonblade.com/2014/03/12/lesbian-judicial-nominee-sails-hearing/

Please Note: Because of the rapid change and growth of technology, web addresses listed in the notes that were valid during research could change or no longer be valid years after this work is published.